Cooking with Jams and Chutneys

Recipes from
Beth's Farm Kitchen

Beth Linskey

Copyright © 2011 Beth Linskey
All rights reserved.

Designed and illustrated by Kerstin Vogdes Diehn
Cover photographs by Krista Bonura
Produced by Symons Brown, Inc.
Manufactured in the USA by GFI Communications Corp.

ISBN 978-0-615-41357-0

For more information, contact bfk@bethsfarmkitchen.com
1 2 3 4 5 6 7 8 9 0

Table of Contents

Introduction 3

Thank You! 9

Jams and More: A Primer 11

Chutneys 27

Zany Jellies, Pickles and Then Some 69

More Jamming Tips from Beth's Farm Kitchen 83

Glossary 89

Recipe Index 95

Jam Notes 99

2   Cooking with Jams and Chutneys: Recipes from Beth's Farm Kitchen

Introduction

A wise woman once told her protégé, "If you never want to regret work, then do something you love." I heeded that advice after stints as a fashion stylist for a catalog photographer, a buyer for a chain store, and a caterer. In the early 1980s, I became a "jammer" and began to sell my products at the New York City Greenmarket. It was a great move! Everyday I go to work, I'm doing something I love!

The Beginnings of the New York City Greenmarket

The New York City Greenmarket was founded in 1976, by Barry Benepe and Bob Lewis. Their goal was to make it possible for local farmers to sell their produce directly to New Yorkers, giving them access to fresh and nutritious food from their own part of the world.

The establishment of the Greenmarket, which offered produce from New York, New Jersey, Connecticut, Pennsylvania, and New England, led to a healthy dialogue among farmers and customers about society's wants, needs, and ability to provide for itself. Farmers learned more about their land and what it could produce; customers learned to enjoy the bounty of their region.

We also learned from each other. The unique requirements of the Greenmarket generated a relationship between buyer and seller that fostered the growth of family farms. The face of regional agriculture changed, with farmers now having a market for perishable "heirloom" crops that were being phased out in favor of "industrialized" crops that looked good and had long shelf lives but lacked personality and integrity.

The Greenmarket has served the city well, and many acres of regional farmland have been saved and improved since Barry and Bob started it.

The Beginnings of Beth's Farm Kitchen

As a caterer, I shopped at the Greenmarket at least once a week and made picture-perfect arrangements of fruits, vegetables and flowers I bought there. When clients asked where to find such gorgeous products, I would say, "Go to the Greenmarket and buy them, but get there early, because caterers and chefs are there first thing."

As a regular Greenmarket shopper, I appreciated the beauty and variety of regional produce, but I also saw a great deal of waste because farmers lacked outlets for their excess produce. City Harvest was in the future. There was a need for a local jam- and pickle-maker.

My great-aunt Agnes made jam and my aunt Mary Antrim was a home economist, but otherwise my family consisted of eaters—not cooks. So I might not have been the ideal person to fill this Greenmarket jam- and pickle-maker opening, but no one else was clamoring for the position, so I took it.

My first attempt at jam-making was in my apartment on Manhattan's Upper West Side. I bought a flat of California strawberries from the Westside Market and some pectin, opened up *The Joy of Cooking*, picked a recipe and tripled it, and a steamy hour later had a beautiful pot of strawberry sauce! This was not an auspicious start, but out of this stumble came Beth's Farm Kitchen.

My business plan was to use locally grown fruits and vegetables to produce jams and jellies in the kitchen of our 1850s farmhouse in the scenic Hudson Valley of New York. I applied to become a vendor at the Greenmarket and undertook recipe research at the New York Public Library. (It was 1980. My first personal computer was a year away, laptops and cell phones were still science fiction, and I doubt Google was even a Stanford M.A.'s dream.)

The New York City Greenmarket and the Slow Food Movement

A lot has changed since I joined the Greenmarket and embraced its commitment to bringing local farm products directly to New York City residents. Today the Greenmarket has many more vendors and offers a greater variety of produce, such as meat, fish, cheese, jams, syrup, honey, pickles and wine. The Greenmarket has grown from a parking lot on Manhattan's East Side to 51 locations throughout the city's five boroughs. It has dedicated local customers and has become an international tourist destination. I know that the mission of the Greenmarket matters.

The Greenmarket's farm-to-market ethic is a forerunner of an approach to eating that challenges and, many believe, is transforming how we buy and consume food. The Slow Food Movement emerged in Italy in 1989 to counteract fast food and fast life. It was a perfect complement to the Greenmarket. The movement is concerned with the disappearance of local food traditions and with the trend of people eating fast food without considering its taste, its nutritional value, or even its source. Thirty years later, there is a whole new vocabulary relating to these topics. Some of its terms include: "locavores," "sustainable agriculture," "100-mile diets and menus," "Community Supported

Agriculture" ("CSA"), "agricultural initiatives," "organic farming," "biodynamic farming," "Integrated Pest Management" ("IPM"), "conventional farming," "low-spray," "No Farms/ No Food," "green revolution," "artisanal," "terroir" and "paleofoods." I am standing on my soap box, or is it an apple box?

Beth's Farm Kitchen Today

The Slow Food Movement also expanded Beth's Farm Kitchen's creative vistas. We produce jams that had been forgotten or lost as culinary resources or remembered only as treats "grandma used to make." These include jams made from green tomatoes, red and black currants, figs, and rhubarb that can now take their place beside standard-bearers such as strawberry and grape jams.

The same logic applies to carrots, corn, beans, ramps, fiddlehead ferns, watermelon rind, and other produce that had long been consigned to garnishing a meal. Now, as pickled products, they stand on their own alongside half-sour dills and bread and butter pickles.

Beth's Farm Kitchen has pushed the envelope further and introduced chutneys made from local produce. We have discovered that locally grown peaches are a viable substitute for sweet mangoes. The more we experiment, the more our customers are willing to test the results and suggest improvements. Most of our taste tests happen in the winter markets. Beth's Farm Kitchen Green Tomato Chutney and Beth's Farm Kitchen Madras Nectar Chutney have come out of these tests. This customer/producer dialogue has created a new collaborative culinary world for us.

The Slow Food Movement revived the word "artisanal," and Beth's Farm Kitchen puts it into practice. We prepare and freeze locally grown fruit in season. We make most of our jams in batches of 12 8-ounce jars. We hand-stir and hand-pour every jar. This is the essence of "artisanal."

Making jam with local fruit has made me only too aware of the trials and tribulations of the small-business owner. The New York Small Scale Food Processors Association (NYSSFPA) makes an effort to encourage new members with advice on marketing, insurance, and licensing regulations. As the local movement catches on, there are many more processors, and I applaud them. As well as being on the Small Scale's board and the association's treasurer, I've recently taken an active role in the Farmer, Consumer Advisory Council (FCAC) of the Greenmarket. After 30 years, it's time to give back.

We want you to make your own jams and chutneys. To help you, we have adjusted our production recipes from 12-jar batches to 4-jar batches and offer suggestions for choosing equipment for safety and convenience, as well as tips for handling fruits and vegetables (see Page 83). You may refrigerate, freeze or can your results. Of course, you can also buy our products in the Greenmarket, at selected retail stores, or through our web site, at www.bethsfarmkitchen.com.

I see my jams and chutneys as an integral part of a family's food experience. Over the years, our culture has lost sight of the importance of meals, and I believe one cause of this has been our need to rush to *finish* meals and the subsequent loss of our desire to *enjoy* them. Our meals, and the ingredients that constitute them, should be a part of our lives. Take the time to make healthful, tasty, beautiful food. Our recipes are nutritious, delicious, visually satisfying, and easy to prepare.

I hope that, as you read this cookbook, you will discover how to integrate jams and chutneys into your meals, improving their taste and increasing your pleasure. Enjoy!

Beth

Thank You!

I could not have produced "Cooking with Jams and Chutneys: Recipes from Beth's Farm Kitchen" alone. Many people contributed to the effort of making this book a reality. I am particularly grateful to ...

... Liz Beals, who helped me take advantage of so many opportunities.

... Charlie Brennan, my partner in eating, planning, and life.

... Mary Anne Symons Brown, my editor, for her patience and perseverance with me. Good thing we both have a sense of humor.

... jammers Linda Romeo, Sacha Eaton, Amanda Schmidt, Margaret Keil, Sharon Smith, Meagan, Donna, Lacey, Nancy, Judy, Kendra, Jen, Jeanie, Sue and many more for their ability to work hard and have fun at the same time.

... testers Jan Linskey, Rosamond Brady, Rosemary Louden, and Anne Wichman, who worked on the chutney chapter energetically.

... my wonderful customers, with whom I have talked for the last 30 years at the Greenmarket about food and family, and who tasted many of the recipes in this book.

... Pat and Jan, tireless proofreaders, rearrangers extraordinaire, brother- and sister-in-law.

... Sharon Brooks, always encouraging with her ability with commas and quotes.

... some of the early influences in my jamming: Laurie McBride, Kathryn Crawford, Kathleen Hunt, and Marcy Goldman.

... friends Doris Jackson, Grace Richardson and many others who have eaten so many meals without complaint and have always had suggestions.

... Gail Bilto and Cindy Lang, who put up with my absence from the market and encouraged me all the way.

... Jennifer Y. Brown, for her sharp editing and her ability to understand Mary Anne and me.

... Skip Skwarek, my very first editor, as well as Maryann Piotrowski and Malega Baldi, for encouraging me along the way.

I am also indebted to many periodicals and books that have informed me over the years, including ...

... The New York Times (for its Wednesday and Sunday food pages).

... Gourmet magazine.

... "Spice," by Jack Turner.

... "The Taste of Conquest," by Michael Krondl.

Jams and More:
A Primer

In 30 years, we at Beth's Farm Kitchen have quite literally boiled our jam recipes down to two styles: with added pectin and without. The better the fruit, the better the jam. Always buy the freshest fruit and use it right away. It's your best guarantee that your jam will have an excellent fresh fruit color and flavor, as well as the right "set" or consistency.

Our pectin of choice is Pomona's Universal Pectin. We have experimented with others, but Pomona's has proven to be the most reliable and consistent in quality and availability. This product suits our style, and we thank its manufacturer. (Pomona's contact information is in the Glossary (Page 89), under "Pectin." Say "hello" to Connie on the company's JAMLINE from Beth's Farm Kitchen.)

Here are some of our most popular Beth's Farm Kitchen products. (See the entire product list online, at www.bethsfarmkitchen.com.)

> **Jams**: Strawberry Rhubarb, Raspberry, Plum, Gingered Pear, Black Currant, Blueberry, Cherrycot

> **Jellies**: Grape, Crabapple, Mint, Red Currant

> **No-Sugar Spreads**: Apple Butter, Chunky Applesauce, and Fruit Spreads

> **Marmalades**: Orange, Meyer Lemon, Triple Fruit

Jams with Added Pectin

Pectin occurs naturally in apples, berries and all other fruits in varying degrees. When heated with sugar, it causes the thickening characteristic of jams. When you do not use added pectin with low-pectin fruits, you must cook them so long that they lose their flavor, color and vitamins. Added pectin speeds up the gelling process, saving time and producing a tastier, healthier, prettier jam. We use citrus-based pectin in our jams.

Beth's Farm Kitchen Basic Jam with Added Pectin

When using Pomona's Universal Pectin, you will need to make "calcium water." Mix 1/2 teaspoon calcium powder (included in pectin box) with 1/2 cup water. Store in refrigerator between uses; it lasts months. Shake well before each use. Discard if settled white powder discolors or molds.

Makes 4 - 5 jars (8-ounce)
Prep Time: 10 minutes   Cook Time: 20 minutes

Ingredients
4 cups whole, chopped or partially mashed fruit
2 teaspoons calcium water
2 cups sugar
2 teaspoons pectin
1/4 cup lemon juice

Directions
Put fruit into medium saucepan. Add calcium water and stir well. In another bowl, thoroughly combine sugar and pectin to avoid clumps of undissolved pectin. Add lemon juice to mixture of fruit and calcium water. Bring to a boil. Slowly pour sugar and pectin mixture into fruit while stirring vigorously. Stir 1 - 2 minutes to dissolve sugar and pectin. Return to a hard boil. Test for set. Remove from heat. Skim if necessary. Pour into sterilized jars or refrigerator containers.

Fruits that Call for Added Pectin

- Strawberries
- Cherries
- Raspberries
- Blueberries
- Blackberries
- Currants
- Gooseberries
- Elderberries

What's What?

Jams: Thick, made with crushed or chopped fruits and sugar.

Jellies: Clear and firm, made with fruit juice and sugar.

Marmalades: Preserves made with citrus fruit, including the rind and pulp, plus sugar.

Conserves: Jams made with two or more fruits, plus either raisins or nuts, or both.

Preserves: Jams made to preserve the shape of the fruit.

Spreads: Beth's Farm Kitchen products made without sugar.

Fruits That Do It on Their Own

- Peaches
- Apricots
- Pears
- Cranberries
- Crabapples
- Rhubarb
- Quince
- Figs
- Plums
- Grapes
- Damson plums
- Nectarines
- Citrus fruits

Jams without Added Pectin

Simple and straightforward. Just keep an eye on the pot, because these jams can stick to the bottom without warning. You get a depth of flavor with this method, but not all fruits work equally well. Cooking time is critical to achieving a spreadable consistency. If the fruit is cooked too long, it can lose its flavor, color, and nutritional value.

Beth's Farm Kitchen Basic Jam without Added Pectin

Makes 4 - 5 jars (8-ounce)
Prep Time: 10 minutes   Cook Time: 45 - 60 minutes

Ingredients
4 cups whole, chopped or partially mashed fruit
1/2 cup (more or less) water
2 cups sugar

Directions
In a medium pot, bring fruit to a simmer. For "drier" fruit, such as cranberries, crabapples and apricots, add 1/2 cup water to fruit to start the cooking. Cook fruit until softened and consistency of thick applesauce. Add sugar and stir regularly on medium heat so bottom of pot does not scorch. When jam has thickened and sheets off a spoon, remove from heat. Skim if necessary. Pour into sterilized jars or refrigerator containers.

Jam drops at first are light and syrupy.

Then they become larger and show signs of sheeting.

When gelling point is reached, jam breaks from spoon in a sheet or flake.

The Fun Begins

I love Serena Bass's jam tarts. Serena has a catering company in New York City and uses our jams. This recipe has become one of her standards.

We also have a common bond, our adorable Westies. Serena's is named Ruby; mine was Jams. Ruby lives on happily in Brooklyn. They enjoyed play dates in the entranceway of Serena's 13th Street kitchen when we made our deliveries.

Jam Tarts

Makes 18 tarts
Prep Time: 35 minutes, plus at least 2 hours for refrigeration
Cook Time: 25 minutes

Ingredients
2 1/2 cups all-purpose flour, plus some for rolling out dough
1 teaspoon salt
2 sticks cold butter, cut into 1/2" cubes
1/2 cup ice-cold water
1 cup **Beth's Farm Kitchen Cherrycot Jam**

Directions
Preheat oven to 350°F. In food processor, combine flour, salt and butter, and pulse 10 times. Add water in a steady stream as you pulse another 10 times. Let crumbs rest for 5 minutes, then place in a plastic bag and gently, but firmly, compress into a 3/4"-thick rectangle. Refrigerate for at least 2 hours.

Remove dough from refrigerator and let sit for 15 minutes to soften slightly before rolling. Put dough on a work surface. Dust top with flour, and sprinkle a good handful of flour underneath, then roll out to a 1/8"-thick rectangle and cut into 3" squares. Using mini-muffin tin, fit one square into each ungreased pocket, leaving 4 corners flat. Carefully place another tin on top and bake for 15 minutes. Remove from oven and lower temperature to 325°F. Allow shells to rest for 1 minute and carefully take off top tin, then fill each shell with 2 teaspoons of **Beth's Farm Kitchen Cherrycot Jam**. Bake for another 10 minutes. Cool before serving.

PB&J Over Time

Age 2: Grape jelly and peanut butter on soft white bread.

Age 6: Strawberry jam, smooth peanut butter on whole wheat bread.

Age 12: Peanut butter, raspberry jam, and banana on rye toast.

Age 18: Chunky peanut butter, blueberry jam on toast.

Age 25: Freshly ground peanut butter, no-sugar spread on whole grain bread.

Age 45: French toast with blueberry jam, mascarpone, and chopped peanuts.

Age 55: Chunky peanut butter, strawberry jam with bacon strips on multigrain bread.

Age 65: Smooth peanut butter, pepper jelly, and saltines.

Age 85: Grape jelly, creamy peanut butter on soft white bread.

Chocolate Frosting

2 tablespoons butter
3/4 cup semi-sweet chocolate chips
6 tablespoons heavy cream
1/2 cup **Beth's Farm Kitchen Black Raspberry Jam**
1 1/4 cups powdered sugar
1 teaspoon vanilla extract

Place all ingredients in a heavy saucepan or a double boiler. Cook over low heat, whisking until smooth. Cool slightly. Add more sugar, if necessary.

This frosting is very spreadable. The leftovers taste like fudge. Yum!

....

Spread the word! You can use jams to fill jelly doughnuts, a favorite trick of Just Rugelach, of the Greenmarket, or as a filling between luscious cake layers, as done at Two Little Red Hens, a New York City bakery on the East Side.

Delectably Dark Chocolate Cake

I did time in the catering world, where I learned to make this "no fail" cake. It dresses up well with flowers. Lilies are my favorite because they complement the rich color of chocolate.

Makes 12 servings
Prep Time: 40 minutes   *Cook Time: 40 - 50 minutes*

Ingredients
1 cup boiling water
3 ounces unsweetened chocolate
1/2 cup butter
1 teaspoon vanilla extract
2 cups sugar
2 eggs, separated
1/2 cup **Beth's Farm Kitchen Black Raspberry Jam**
1 teaspoon baking soda
1/2 cup sour cream
2 cups all-purpose flour
1 teaspoon baking powder

Directions
Preheat oven to 350°F. Grease and flour a 10" Bundt pan. Knock out excess flour.

In a medium bowl, pour water over chocolate and butter; let stand until melted. Stir in vanilla extract and sugar, then whisk in egg yolks. Add **Beth's Farm Kitchen Black Raspberry Jam**.

In another bowl, mix baking soda and sour cream; whisk into chocolate mixture. Sift flour and baking powder together and add to batter, mixing thoroughly.

Beat egg whites until stiff but not dry. Stir 1 large spoonful of whipped egg whites thoroughly into batter and gently fold in rest of egg whites. Pour batter into prepared pan; bake for 40 - 50 minutes, or until edges pull away from sides of pan. Cool in pan for 10 minutes. Unmold and cool completely before frosting.

Jams and More: A Primer   15

Nancy's Rhubarb Coffee Cake

Nancy Allen worked in our kitchen for years and had a wonderful repertoire of cake delights for us. The Kitchen Jammers use any excuse to make a cake, and this is one of our favorites.

Makes 12 servings
Prep Time: 20 minutes   Cook Time: 40 - 50 minutes

Ingredients
1 package yellow cake mix
2/3 cup packed brown sugar
2 tablespoons butter
3/4 cup chopped walnuts
2 eggs
1 cup sour cream
1 cup **Beth's Farm Kitchen Raspybarb Jam**

Directions
Preheat oven to 350°F. In a small bowl, combine 2/3 cup cake mix and sugar. Cut in butter until crumbly. Add walnuts. Set aside. Place remaining cake mix (3 cups) in another bowl. Add eggs and sour cream. Fold in **Beth's Farm Kitchen Raspybarb Jam**. Spread on greased 13" x 9" x 2" baking pan. Sprinkle with prepared crumb mixture. Bake for 40 - 50 minutes, or until toothpick inserted near center comes out clean. Cool on wire rack. Serve.

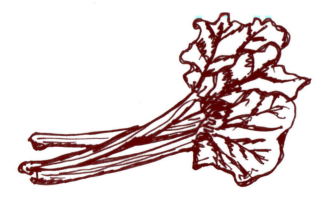

Rhubarb: Fascinating Facts

- Cultivated in China as early as 2700 B.C.
- One of the treasures of the Silk Road. It came from Nepal.
- It's a vegetable, not a fruit.
- Part of buckwheat family, related to garden sorrel.
- Crisp stalks, bright pink to reddish, are sweetest; green varieties are more tart.
- Only stalks are edible. Leaves are toxic in quantities of a bushel or more.
- Good source of vitamin C, calcium and dietary fiber.
- Cultivated for medicinal purposes.
- June 9 is National Strawberry-Rhubarb Pie Day.

Jammy Baked Apples

Preheat oven to 375°F. Place 4 Cortland apples, peeled and cored, in a pie pan. Stuff each apple with 1/2 tablespoon butter and 1 tablespoon **Beth's Farm Kitchen Blackberry Jam**. Bake, basting occasionally, until apples are very tender and glazed, for about 1 hour.

Serve warm or at room temperature, topped with crème fraîche, sour cream, or yogurt.

Orange on Orange Sweet Loaf

Adapted from a recipe created by Deb Gavito for Body and Soul, her vegetarian bakery in the Greenmarket. (She also owns Counter, in New York City's East Village.)

Makes 1 loaf
Prep Time: 30 minutes   Cook Time: 50 - 60 minutes

Ingredients
1 cup all-purpose flour
1 cup whole wheat flour
1 teaspoon baking soda
1 teaspoon baking powder
1/4 teaspoon ground cinnamon
1/4 teaspoon grated fresh nutmeg
1/4 teaspoon grated fresh mace
1/4 teaspoon grated fresh ginger
1/4 teaspoon sea salt
1 cup sweet potato baked until soft, peeled and mashed
1/2 cup packed light brown sugar
1/4 cup orange juice
1/4 cup silken tofu
1 cup **Beth's Farm Kitchen Apricot Jam**

Directions
Preheat oven to 325°F. Mix and sift all dry ingredients in a medium bowl. Blend sweet potato, light brown sugar, orange juice, tofu and **Beth's Farm Kitchen Apricot Jam** in a food processor until smooth. Combine liquid and dry ingredients. Pour batter into greased bread pan. Bake for approximately 1 hour. Test with a toothpick. If it comes out clean, it is done. Let cool. Slice and serve. Extraordinary when toasted!

Jams and More: A Primer

Aunt Gilda's Plum Crumb Cake

This comes from the family of Liz Beals, Beth's Farm Kitchen's Chief Jammer. To Liz, food and family are synonymous.

Makes 6 - 8 servings
Prep Time: 20 minutes   Cook Time: 1 hour

Ingredients
1 1/2 cups all-purpose flour
1/2 cup sugar
1 teaspoon baking powder
4 ounces softened butter, plus enough for buttering pan
1 cup chopped walnuts (optional)
1 egg, whisked
1 cup **Beth's Farm Kitchen Plum Jam**

Directions
Preheat oven to 400°F. Butter a square, 8" x 8" pan. Mix flour, sugar and baking powder and cut butter into dry mixture until a fine crumb forms. Mix in walnuts (optional). With fork, stir in egg until large crumbs form. Leave it loose and don't overmix. Divide crumb mixture into two equal portions. Firmly press one portion of crumb into bottom and sides of pan. Spread **Beth's Farm Kitchen Plum Jam** on top of pressed crumb layer. Sprinkle second portion of crumb mixture on top of jam layer. Leave loose. Bake at 400°F for 15 minutes. You may want to place a larger sheet pan on rack below the tray so drippings don't burn in bottom of oven. After 15 minutes, lower oven temperature to 350°F and bake for 40 - 45 minutes, until golden brown. Remove pan from oven and let cool completely so cake will set. Cut and serve when cool.

Plum Types Grown in Northeastern U.S.

We use the oval, dark blue or purple, freestone varieties: Stanley, Italian, Fellenburg, President, Empress, Valor, Long John, Castleton.

Damson plums are small and tart and make great jam. Joe Nicholson of Red Jacket Orchards told me his mom had a single tree in her front yard. That prolific tree supplied us for years.

Beach plums are native to the Northeast Coast of the U.S. They need sand dunes to prosper. We planted 4 bushes behind our barn and over many years they produced only 40 jars of jam. That upstate New York barn needs a sand dune!

Mirabelle plums should grow in the Northeast, but I have never found them here. If you find them, please e-mail bfk@bethsfarmkitchen.com.

Duck Breasts with Chutney and Jam

Preheat oven to 350°F. Score skin of 2 boneless duck breasts. Rub with salt and pepper. Sear breasts in skillet, 2 minutes per side. Pour off rendered fat. Roast 15 - 20 minutes.

Sauce

Melt 2 tablespoons butter in skillet and add 1/2 cup minced onions or shallots. Sauté until translucent. Add 1 cup beef broth and 1 cup red wine. Reduce by half. Add 1/4 cup **Beth's Farm Kitchen Quincherry Chutney**, 1/4 teaspoon rosemary. Stir. Pour into blender. Blend 10 - 15 seconds. Return sauce to pan. Add 1/2 cup **Beth's Farm Kitchen Sour Cherry Jam**. Stir. Add salt and freshly ground black pepper to taste. Simmer. Remove duck breasts from oven, transfer to plates, keep warm. Add sauce to baking pan to deglaze. Pour over duck breasts and serve with polenta and asparagus. Elegant!

Lemon Blueberry Pie

This is a luscious lemony tart and, since my favorite color is blue, we usually use **Beth's Farm Kitchen Blueberry Jam** for an absolutely perfect finishing touch. Apricot is another of my favorite choices. Use your imagination and any Beth's Farm Kitchen jam to make an extra-special treat.

Makes 8 servings
Prep Time: 45 minutes, plus 1 hour for refrigeration
Cook Time: 20 minutes

Ingredients
1 premade, refrigerated pie crust
2 tablespoons finely chopped pecans
1/2 cup sugar
2 tablespoons cornstarch
1/2 cup water
2 tablespoons butter
1 egg yolk, beaten
1/3 cup lemon juice
1 cup **Beth's Farm Kitchen Blueberry Jam**

Directions

Preheat oven to 450°F. Shape and press crust into pie pan. Generously prick entire crust with a fork. Add pecans and press into crust. Bake 9 - 11 minutes, or until golden brown. Cool completely. In small saucepan, combine sugar and cornstarch. Stir in water, butter, and egg yolk. Cook over medium heat until mixture boils and thickens, stirring constantly. Boil for 1 minute. Remove from heat. Stir in lemon juice. Pour into cooled crust. Refrigerate for 1 hour. Spread **Beth's Farm Kitchen Blueberry Jam** gently on top of custard. Chill pie again and serve cold with whipped cream.

Jams and More: A Primer

Ginger Peachy Clafoutis

Clafoutis. The name is so mysterious, so pretty. It originated in the Limousin region of France, where it is made with sweet or tart cherries. We make it with **Beth's Farm Kitchen Gingered Peach Jam**. The combination is heavenly. Choose your favorite jam and make this easy brunch dish with it.

Makes 8 servings
Prep Time: 10 minutes   Cook Time: 40 minutes

Ingredients
1/4 cup butter
2 eggs
1 egg yolk
1/2 cup sugar
Pinch of salt
1/2 cup all-purpose flour
1 cup milk
1 cup **Beth's Farm Kitchen Gingered Peach Jam**
2 teaspoons powdered sugar

Directions
Preheat oven to 375°F. Melt butter in small saucepan. Let cool slightly. Combine and blend all ingredients, except jam and powdered sugar. Pour into a greased pie pan. Swirl **Beth's Farm Kitchen Gingered Peach Jam** into batter. Bake for 40 minutes. Let cool for 5 minutes; dust with powdered sugar. Serve warm. The puff deflates somewhat when taken out of the oven; it's supposed to!

Christian's Sautéed Shrimp

For years and years in the Greenmarket, we had only Jam Ma'ams and Martin's Pretzels had Pretzel Boys. A few years ago, we integrated a bit, so we have had two Pretzel Boys working with us, and Christian is now a Jam Man, as well as a cook. This recipe is his invention.

Combine 1 pound shrimp or scallops with 4 pieces of **Beth's Farm Kitchen Cherry Peppers**, medium dice, in preheated sauté pan with 2 tablespoons olive oil. Sauté for 2 minutes, or until just about cooked. Add 1/2 cup **Beth's Farm Kitchen Gingered Pear Jam** and chopped cilantro. Stir. Heat through and serve over baked smashed plantains or yellow rice. Enjoy!

Cooking with Jams and Chutneys: Recipes from Beth's Farm Kitchen

Who is Charlie?

Charlie Brennan is my husband and the inventor of **Beth's Farm Kitchen Blazing Tomato Chutney**; he has made many a peach cobbler. Anyone who visited our house in the 1980s and 1990s had peach cobbler for dessert and again for breakfast. The Jammers froze peaches and put his name on the bags, and no one dared use those peaches.

Our nieces and nephews remember eating hot cobblers with vanilla ice cream. This recipe is a little walk down Memory Lane.

Fruit Favorites

Cobbler, crumble, crisp, slump and grunt, buckle, brown betty, pandowdy, crunch, dumpling, küchen, turnover, clafoutis, upside-down cake, flaugnarde: These are all cooked with fruit in, on or under a pastry crust.

Peach Jam Cobbler

Adapted from Charlie Brennan's cobbler recipe. Cobbler is a simple, traditional family dessert. It can be made with peaches, blueberries, blackberries, or your favorite Beth's Farm Kitchen jams.

Makes 6 servings
Prep Time: 15 minutes   Cook Time: 20 minutes

Ingredients
2 cups **Beth's Farm Kitchen Peach Jam**
6 tablespoons softened butter
1/4 cup packed light brown sugar
Lemon or lime zest
1 cup all-purpose flour
Pinch of salt (optional)

Directions
Preheat oven to 350°F. Pour **Beth's Farm Kitchen Peach Jam** into a pie pan. Combine remaining ingredients, mixing thoroughly. Drop mixture by spoonfuls (pea to gumball size) onto jam. Bake for 20 minutes.

Serve warm with cream or ice cream. Leftovers make a great breakfast. This is an easy winter dessert when fresh fruit is out of season.

Spreads: No Sugar Added

There has always been a demand for products with no sugar added. We originally made them for diabetics, but as food styles changed, more and more people became aware that no-sugar products had health benefits and could taste good.

Beth's Farm Kitchen decided not to use sugar substitutes or concentrated juices. We went with ground-up apples. This adds flavor, texture, pectin and plump to the main fruit. We like the result, but even though we "can" these products, they will not last more than 8 weeks in a refrigerator, opened or not. The shelf life of these products is the same as that of a piece of fruit in your refrigerator. Remember, sugar is a preservative, and we are not adding any.

Oh, and by the way, we call our no-sugar products "spreads" to distinguish them from jams, which are made with sugar.

Beth's Farm Kitchen Basic No-Sugar Spread

Makes 4 - 5 jars (8-ounce)
Prep Time: 1 hour   *Cook Time: 45 minutes*

Ingredients
4 cups partially chopped or mashed fruit
1 1/2 cups peeled apples, puréed
1 tablespoon lemon juice

Directions
Place ingredients in saucepan and cook until juices have evaporated. Pour into sterilized jars or refrigerator containers.

Fruits We Use in Spreads

- Apples
- Apricots
- Blackberries
- Blueberries
- Peaches
- Plums
- Pears
- Raspberries
- Strawberries
- Sour cherries

A Few Ways to Use Spreads

There is always the toast option. You can also:

- Spread on rice cakes
- Mix with granola.
- Put on ice cream.
- Freeze and use as a sorbet.
- Semi-freeze as a granita.
- Add to yogurt.
- Eat directly from jar.

Pork Glaze with Beth's Farm Kitchen Apple Butter

This is a great variation on glazes. Combine equal parts **Beth's Farm Kitchen Apple Butter**, mustard, and dark ale. Slather over pork loin. Roast at 350°F for 20 minutes per pound, until golden brown. Baste meat every 10 minutes. This recipe also works well with chicken and duck breasts.

Beth's Farm Kitchen Basic Chunky Applesauce

Warm **Beth's Farm Kitchen Chunky Applesauce** and serve with ice cream or frozen yogurt for dessert. I have even added just a squirt of chocolate sauce and a dollop of lemon curd. When time is tight, we use a ready-made pie crust and spread 4 cups of applesauce on top of pie crust. Bake in 350°F oven until warm and serve. Frozen yogurt will keep the calories down. But first, make your own delicious applesauce with this recipe.

Makes 4 - 5 jars (8-ounce)
Prep Time: 30 minutes   Cook Time: 15 minutes

Ingredients
2 apples, peeled, cored and cubed
2 apples, peeled, cored and puréed
1 teaspoon cinnamon
Dash of nutmeg
1 teaspoon lemon juice
1/4 cup each dark and golden raisins

Directions
Combine ingredients in a medium saucepan and bring to a simmer over medium heat. Simmer until cubed apples are soft. Pour into jars or refrigerator containers. Serve warm or cold, for breakfast or as a snack, in jar or out.

Marmalades: The Not-So-Local Ingredients

Marmalades are not made with fruits grown in the Northeast, so the jam-makers of the New York City Greenmarket had to do some convincing to get the Greenmarket to agree to include marmalades in our jam mix. We succeeded, and we make great coarse-cut marmalades. Our citrus fruits are purchased in January, the high season in California, Arizona, and Florida for oranges, grapefruit, Sevilles, blood oranges, Meyer lemons, and bitter oranges. We have been told that these bitter oranges make a great marinade for grilled chicken or duck. Sounds good and, of course, they make tasty marms.

Beth's Farm Kitchen Orange Marmalade

Makes 7 jars (8-ounce)
Prep Time: 30 minutes, plus overnight for refrigeration
Cook Time: 45 - 60 minutes

Ingredients
4 oranges
2 lemons
10 cups water
6 cups sugar

Directions
Slice fruit whole, rind and all. In a large bowl, combine fruit with water. Refrigerate overnight. In a large pot, bring fruit and water to a simmer over medium heat. When half of water has evaporated, remove seeds, add sugar, and cook until marmalade is at the "soft ball" stage. This means that, when you drop a teaspoon of cooking marmalade into a jar of cold water, marmalade looks like a soft candy ball rather than dispersing or forming a hard ball. A candy thermometer will read 235 - 245°F. Pour remainder of marmalade into sterilized jars or refrigerator containers.

Soaking and Freezing Citrus Fruits

Do not skip soaking citrus fruits overnight when making traditional coarse-cut marmalade. This step allows the natural pectin to be pulled out of the rind so that, when you cook the marmalade, you will get a lovely, soft set.

Another option that Beth's Farm Kitchen Jammers discovered is to slice the fruit and freeze it for later use. When Sevilles are in season, we buy enough for the year and make batches as we need them. I thought this was brilliant!

Sweet Memories of Palachinka

Before I ever even thought of starting Beth's Farm Kitchen, I had a dessert at The Red Tulip on East 83rd Street in Manhattan that has stuck in my memory. There was always a line to get into this restaurant, but I could usually get someone to go with me at 10 p.m., and we would get seated right away and just have palachinka, a crêpe with jam and powdered sugar. It was marvelous. You can make your own palachinka with this crêpe recipe and **Beth's Farm Kitchen Raspberry Jam** or **Beth's Farm Kitchen Sour Cherry Jam**.

Crêpes Suzette à la Beth's Farm Kitchen

Makes 6 - 10 crêpes
Prep Time: 15 minutes, plus overnight for refrigeration
Cook Time: 15 minutes

Ingredients
For Crêpes
3/4 cup milk
3/4 cup water
2 eggs
1 egg yolk
2 tablespoons **Beth's Farm Kitchen Orange Marmalade**
1 cup all-purpose flour
5 tablespoons softened butter

For Suzette Mixture
1 cup orange juice
1/2 cup **Beth's Farm Kitchen Orange Marmalade**
3 tablespoons softened butter

Directions
For Crêpes
Combine ingredients in blender. Blend for 10 - 15 seconds. Strain batter through fine sieve and refrigerate overnight.

Heat a well-seasoned crêpe pan or use a non-stick pan. Scoop 2 ounces of chilled batter into pan; tilt pan to spread the batter evenly. Cook one side. Flip it, and cook other side. Stack cooked crêpes and cover with dish towel to keep warm and moist.

For Suzette Mixture
Simmer orange juice until reduced by half. Mash **Beth's Farm Kitchen Orange Marmalade** with butter. Whisk with orange juice until blended. Fold crêpes in quarters, dip into sauce, and serve.

A Good Idea: Crêpes freeze beautifully. Make a batch and freeze with waxed paper between individual crêpes. Reheat in a non-stick pan.

Jams and More: A Primer   25

Saucy Pork Cutlets

Flying Pigs Farm is a fellow vendor in the Union Square Greenmarket. We often pick their brains for new ways to use their excellent pork products with our chutneys. This is one of their best ideas ever.

Makes 4 servings
Prep Time: 20 minutes, plus 1 hour to overnight for marinating
Cook Time: 10 minutes

Ingredients
1 pound pork (fresh ham) cutlets, pounded thin
1 cup **Beth's Farm Kitchen Chili Cranberry Chutney**, puréed
Coarse salt and freshly ground black pepper to taste
1/4 cup all-purpose flour
1/4 cup olive oil
1/4 cup dry white wine
1/2 teaspoon soy sauce
2 minced garlic cloves
1/2 cup **Beth's Farm Kitchen Meyer Lemon Marmalade**

Directions
Place cutlets and **Beth's Farm Kitchen Chili Cranberry Chutney** in plastic bag. Marinate for 1 hour to overnight. Remove cutlets from marinade.

Add salt and pepper to flour. Dust cutlets. Shake off excess.

Heat skillet with 2 tablespoons olive oil. Add pork, sauté 2 minutes per side, until just barely cooked through. Transfer pork to platter and keep warm.

Add 2 tablespoons olive oil, wine and soy sauce to skillet and continue heating until skillet is deglazed.

Add garlic and **Beth's Farm Kitchen Meyer Lemon Marmalade**. Sauté 30 seconds to 1 minute, whisking gently.

Add salt and pepper to taste. Pour over cutlets and serve.

The soy balances the flavor and cuts the sweetness. The side dish I recommend is a corn, tomato, and cilantro sauté sprinkled with parmesan cheese. Pretty plate.

Tangy Marinade for Chicken or Lamb Chops

1/2 cup olive oil
1/2 cup **Beth's Farm Kitchen Bitter Orange Marmalade**
1/4 cup white wine
1 tablespoon lemon juice
1 clove garlic, minced
3 teaspoons fresh rosemary
Salt and pepper, to taste

Combine ingredients in blender. Pulse 10 seconds. Marinate chicken or lamb chops for 30 minutes before grilling.

Chutneys

The word "chutney" comes from a Hindi word meaning "to crush" or "to lick" and refers to a savory condiment. Beth's Farm Kitchen chutneys are made from a combination of fruits, vegetables, sugar, vinegar and spices. Chutneys of this type are known as "English-style," made both in England and in India, where the English were first introduced to chutneys. There are many other chutney styles, however, encompassing a broad range of ingredients and flavors.

We hope that chutneys become an integral part of your diet. They will delight your taste buds!

Chutney Ingredients, from Around the World
These, and many more, have traveled far.

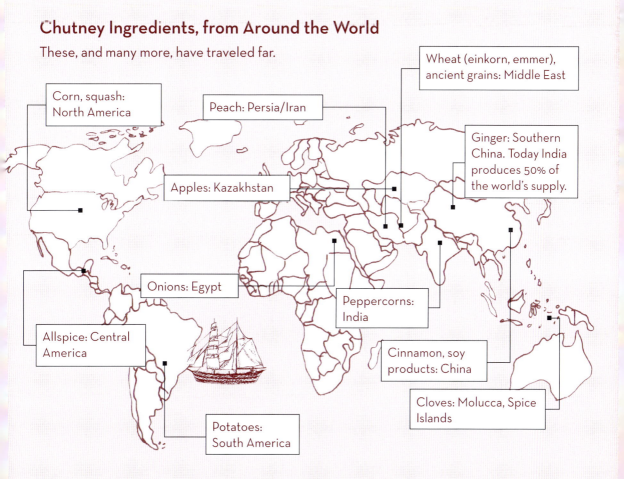

- Corn, squash: North America
- Peach: Persia/Iran
- Wheat (einkorn, emmer), ancient grains: Middle East
- Apples: Kazakhstan
- Ginger: Southern China. Today India produces 50% of the world's supply.
- Onions: Egypt
- Peppercorns: India
- Allspice: Central America
- Cinnamon, soy products: China
- Cloves: Molucca, Spice Islands
- Potatoes: South America

Beth's Farm Kitchen Chutneys, from Hot to Sweet

Beth's Farm Kitchen's chutneys vary in spiciness. In our hottest offerings, we use habanero peppers; in our mildest, cinnamon and cloves are key ingredients. Try one, or try them all!

For our maximum kick:
> Ragin' Rhubarb
> Bellow Yellow

A little more civilized:
> Blazing Tomato™
> Hot Plum
> Cranberry Horseradish
> Zapricot
> Chili Cranberry
> Green Tomato
> Hot 'n' Spicy

More mellow:
> Rhubarb
> Madras Nectar
> Golden Pear
> Peach

No heat added:
> Cranberry Lime
> Quincherry
> Plum
> Delta Road

On to the recipes …

Reminiscences

As a kid in Chicago, I never saw a more exotic condiment than ketsup at home; Milwaukee was far away, so mustard wasn't in our family's lexicon.

Mom did serve anchovy paste mixed with cream cheese on celery, though, so we were not totally deprived!

We also had two kinds of fish on Fridays—Mrs. Paul's fish sticks, and tuna noodle casserole with potato-chip topping.

....

I have been a long-time listener of "A Prairie Home Companion," with Garrison Keillor. So, I like to say that **Beth's Farm Kitchen Blazing Tomato Chutney™** is "the Ketsup of Chutneyland": It has "natural mellowing agents."

Beth's Farm Kitchen Blazing Tomato Chutney™

My business began with jam-making, but, early on, I spent many hours in the New York Public Library reading old cookbooks about the origins of chutneys. This is Beth's Farm Kitchen's first original chutney recipe.

Makes 3 - 4 jars (8-ounce)
Prep Time: 30 minutes   Cook Time: 45 - 60 minutes

Ingredients
14 ounces tomato juice*
1 cup granulated sugar
1 medium onion, small dice
1 clove garlic, chopped
2 tablespoons fresh ginger, chopped
2 tablespoons jalapeño peppers, chopped
1 tablespoon sambal oelek, or to taste
1 tablespoon, plus 2 teaspoons, whole mustard seeds
1 tablespoon red pepper flakes
1 teaspoon ground allspice
3/4 cup cider vinegar
1/2 cup red bell pepper, small dice
1/2 cup green bell pepper, small dice
1 Ida Red apple, peeled, cored, small dice
1 Granny Smith apple, peeled, cored, small dice
1/4 cup sliced almonds

Directions
Combine all ingredients, except apples and almonds, in a medium saucepan. Cook over medium heat, stirring frequently, for 30 - 45 minutes, or until thickened. Add apples and cook until they soften. Stir in almonds. Remove from heat and pour hot into sterilized jars or refrigerator containers.

* We make our own tomato juice, and you can, too. Just place 1 pound cored tomatoes in blender or food processor and purée until smooth. A 1-quart freezer bag holds 14 ounces. (During tomato season, we make the juice and then freeze it for later use.)

Chutneys   29

Cowboy Chili

Beth's Farm Kitchen Blazing Tomato Chutney™ gives depth and richness of flavor to this recipe. The chili is also great the next day.

Makes 4 - 6 servings
Prep Time: 20 minutes   Cook Time: 1 hour and 10 minutes

Ingredients
3 tablespoons olive oil
2 pounds ground meat (beef, veal, pork, turkey, or any combination of these)
1 onion (medium to large), roughly chopped
1 can (16-ounce) diced tomatoes
1 can (14.5-ounce) diced tomatoes with chili
1 cup **Beth's Farm Kitchen Blazing Tomato Chutney™**
1/4 cup Katchkie Ketchup
1 can (15.5-ounce) red beans, undrained (optional)
1 tablespoon chili powder
2 teaspoons ground cumin
Sea salt and freshly ground black pepper, to taste

Directions
Cover the bottom of a soup pot with a thin film of olive oil. Cook over medium heat until oil is hot but not smoking. Add meat and onion; cook, stirring until meat is no longer pink and onion is softened. Drain excess grease. Add tomatoes and stir well to deglaze pot. Add **Beth's Farm Kitchen Blazing Tomato Chutney™**, ketsup, beans (optional) and spices, stirring to combine. Bring to a boil, then reduce heat to a simmer and continue to cook for 1 hour. Adjust seasoning. Serve in bowls with sour cream, chopped onions, red peppers, or grated cheese.

Fish Story Retold

The first time I had fish cooked this way was at my parents' home in East Orleans.

My sister Susie and I had been sailing my tiny Snark and, on our walk up from the bay, with the boat over our heads, a neighbor tossed into the boat a fish he had just caught. He knew Dad would be envious, because, no matter how hard he tried, Dad could not catch a fish. Dad did not believe we had caught the fish ourselves, while out on the Snark, and did not take the bait, but he happily filleted the fish.

The following is how Dad taught us to cook the fish (bluefish), and I have used this recipe happily for many meaty fish, such as cod and halibut.

Cut two sheets heavy-duty aluminum foil for each fillet, making sure they are about 4" longer than the fillet.

Lay each fillet on foil, skin side down. Place foil on a cookie sheet. Rub each fillet with 1/3 cup **Beth's Farm Kitchen Blazing Tomato Chutney™**; then sprinkle each fillet with 1/4 cup scallions, 1/2 chopped tomato, 1/4 cup chopped red pepper, 1/4 cup chopped cilantro, and season with freshly ground black pepper.

Close foil by crimping edges and making a tent-like package. Place cookie sheet in oven and bake at 400°F for 25 minutes. Check for doneness.

Chez Brennan Meatloaf

This recipe calls for 2 pounds of meatloaf mixture, but feel free to cut it in half. Charlie and I usually make a 2-pound loaf because we love leftovers. We buy a meatloaf mixture from the butcher or use 1/2 pound of this, plus 1/2 pound of that. We have used ground beef, veal, turkey and sausage. A friend of ours uses only ground turkey because her family does not eat red meat, and everyone loves the results.

Makes 8 servings
Prep Time: 20 minutes   Cook Time: 45 - 60 minutes

Ingredients
2 pounds meatloaf mixture
1/2 cup bread crumbs (dry, seasoned, or fresh)
1 egg
1 onion, medium dice
1 cup **Beth's Farm Kitchen Blazing Tomato Chutney™**
1/2 cup corn or peas
1/2 cup chopped parsley
1/2 cup grated carrots
1/4 cup grated parmesan cheese
Freshly ground black pepper
1 can (8-ounce) tomato sauce

Directions
Preheat oven to 350°F. Place all ingredients, except pepper and tomato sauce, in a large bowl and knead together. Season with pepper. Pour mixture into a cast-iron skillet and shape into a mound. Pour tomato sauce over meatloaf. Bake for 45 - 60 minutes, basting twice during cooking.

Remove from oven and let set for 10 minutes. Slice and serve with garlic mashed potatoes and a green salad.

Chutneys   31

Spaghetti Puttanesca

Many a dinner is a fast and furious event in our house. But, I just love to sit down and talk and eat, a result of my upbringing. This is one of the "it takes no time at all" recipes that taste good and allow plenty of talk time.

Makes 4 servings
Prep Time: 15 minutes   *Cook Time: 15 - 20 minutes*

Ingredients
2 ounces pancetta, medium dice
1/2 onion, medium dice
2 cloves garlic, minced
1 tablespoon olive oil
6 fresh plum tomatoes, chopped
1 cup **Beth's Farm Kitchen Blazing Tomato Chutney™**
2 tablespoons capers
1/4 cup Kalamata olives, sliced
1/4 cup chopped parsley
1 pound spaghetti
Grated parmesan cheese, for garnish

Directions
For Sauce
Sauté pancetta, onion and garlic in oil over medium heat. Add tomatoes and **Beth's Farm Kitchen Blazing Tomato Chutney™**, and simmer for 15 minutes. Add capers, olives and parsley and stir. Set aside.

For Pasta
While sauce is simmering, boil water and cook spaghetti. When pasta is ready, add 2 or 3 tablespoons of pasta water to the sauce. Drain spaghetti and add to saucepan, or plate pasta and pour sauce over it. Add parmesan and serve.

Market Talk

What can you do with **Beth's Farm Kitchen Blazing Tomato Chutney™**?

- In the morning, add to scrambled egg sandwich.

- Make a superior grilled cheese: Spread on bread, top with cheese, and grill.

- Serve with cheddar and salami.

- Mix with plain yogurt for veggie dip.

- Use to marinate tofu.

- Add to a sauté of Swiss chard, mushrooms and tomatoes.

- Serve with sardines and crackers.

- Top fried polenta with it.

- Add to quesadillas with chicken and arugula.

- Include in Bloody Mary mix.

- Stir into a creamy salad dressing.

- Use as a stuffed-pepper helper.

- Mix into chicken or tomato soup for added depth of flavor.

- Layer into lasagna.

- Make tamales with it.

- Use to doctor your marinara or meat sauce.

- Add to a stew that needs a zesty tang.

- Use to marinate shrimp; then grill.

- Use to top off grilled steaks and burgers.

- Mix with spicy corn relish for a hot dog topper.

- Spread on a warm biscuit with parmesan.

- Add to picadillo for more flavor.

- Use as a savory touch for empanadas.

- Enrich lean burger meat with it.

- Add to mac 'n' cheese.

Pasta e Fagioli Soup

A thick crusty bread and a chilly day complete this hearty soup.

Makes 4 - 6 servings
Prep Time: 45 minutes   Cook Time: 30 minutes

Ingredients
4 ounces ditalini pasta
Olive oil
1 garlic clove
1 potato, large dice
1 medium zucchini, large dice
5 ounces green beans, chopped
1 can (12-ounce) diced tomatoes
1 can (8-ounce) chickpeas or white beans, drained
1 cup **Beth's Farm Kitchen Blazing Tomato Chutney™**
2 quarts water
2 cups fresh spinach, chopped*
Sea salt and freshly ground pepper
Grated parmesan cheese, for garnish

Directions
Cook pasta until al dente; drain and set aside. In a soup pot, heat oil and sauté garlic until golden. Add potato, zucchini, green beans, tomatoes, chickpeas or white beans, and **Beth's Farm Kitchen Blazing Tomato Chutney™** and stir. Add water to thin mixture to a soup consistency. Simmer 25 minutes to combine flavors. Add spinach and pasta. Cook another 5 minutes, stirring so pasta does not stick to pan. Taste and adjust seasoning. Ladle into bowls and top with cheese.

Serve with warm Italian bread and a green salad.

* You can use greens other than spinach, such as Swiss chard or escarole.

Chutneys   33

Savory Gruyère Clafoutis

This is similar to the clafoutis in the jam chapter (on Page 20), but it is savory instead of sweet. It came to us from Jan Linskey, a sister-in-law. The first time I served this dish was for brunch, but it works equally well for dinner with a salad, or cut into small slices as an appetizer.

Makes 6 servings
Prep Time: 15 minutes   Cook Time: 20 - 25 minutes

Ingredients
3 eggs
1/2 cup milk
1/2 cup all-purpose flour
1/4 teaspoon sea salt
Freshly ground black pepper, to taste
1/2 cup **Beth's Farm Kitchen Blazing Tomato Chutney™**
3/4 cup grated Gruyère cheese
1 - 2 tablespoons butter, to coat pan

Directions
Preheat oven to 400°F. Combine eggs, milk, flour, salt and pepper in bowl and beat until smooth. Stir in **Beth's Farm Kitchen Blazing Tomato Chutney™** and cheese. Melt butter in large cast-iron skillet. Swirl to coat sides, and pour in batter. Bake until puffed and golden brown, approximately 20 - 25 minutes. Serve hot or at room temperature.

Breezy Brisket

As you are about to leave for the office or drop the kids off at day care, pull out the slow cooker and set up dinner for tonight. (It actually takes more planning than that, I realize).

Put 1 cup **Beth's Farm Kitchen Blazing Tomato Chutney™** and 1 cup tomato juice in cooker; mix. Add 3 - 4 pounds brisket (stew meat or pot roast also works). Set cooker for 8 hours, or for as much time as necessary according to manufacturer's instructions.

When you return, transfer meat to a platter and cover. Separate excess fat from cooking liquid. Adjust seasoning with sea salt and freshly ground black pepper. Slice brisket, serve with cooking liquid, steamed gingered carrots, and wide egg noodles. Easy, breezy and tasty!

Pears on Parade

I came late to my love of pears, but I have embraced them. They look and taste luscious.

Bartlett's: Soft and sweet, pale green to light yellow when ripe.

Bosc: Firm, not sweet, until after frost, holds shape when baked and poached. Used in **Beth's Farm Kitchen Golden Pear Chutney** and **Beth's Farm Kitchen Gingered Pear Jam**.

Clapp's Favorite: Mouthwateringly delicious when ripe.

D'Anjou: The most beautifully shaped and colored.

Seckel: Small, crisp, firm, sweet; usually canned whole.

Asian: Apple-shaped and pear-textured.

Comice: Sweet and round, most common pear in gift baskets.

Beth's Farm Kitchen Golden Pear Chutney

We spent many days and tossed out many batches selecting the best pear for our chutney. The winner was Bosc. A warning: Be aware that late Bartlett's pears just turn to mush!

Makes 3 - 4 jars (8-ounce)
Prep Time: 45 minutes   Cook Time: 30 - 45 minutes

Ingredients
4 cups pears, peeled, cored, and sliced
1/2 cup granulated sugar
1/2 cup golden raisins
1/3 cup cider vinegar
1/2 cup red bell pepper, small dice
3 tablespoons fresh chopped ginger
1/2 medium onion, small dice
1 hot red cherry pepper, chopped
1/4 teaspoon ground cayenne pepper
1/4 cup sliced almonds

Directions
Combine all ingredients, except almonds, in a medium saucepan. Cook over medium heat, stirring frequently, for 30 - 45 minutes, or until thickened. Take off heat, stir in almonds, and pour hot into sterilized jars or refrigerator containers.

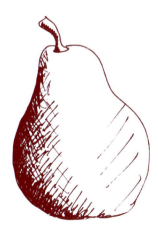

Chutneys 35

Chutney Upside-Down Cake

Growing up, we had many pineapple upside-down cakes. They were always made in a black cast-iron skillet. Did that add to the caramelizing of the brown sugar and butter, or was it the style of the day? Dole promoted pineapple upside-down cake after World War II to get us to eat pineapples, and we did! Serve for brunch with champagne.

Makes 6 - 8 servings
Prep Time: 25 minutes   Cook Time: 40 - 45 minutes

Ingredients
1 cup all-purpose flour
3/4 cup sugar
1 1/2 teaspoons baking powder
1/2 teaspoon salt
1/4 cup melted butter
1/2 cup milk
1 egg
1/4 cup butter
4 cups **Beth's Farm Kitchen Golden Pear Chutney**
1/3 cup sliced almonds, toasted
1 cup heavy cream, whipped

Directions
Preheat oven to 350°F. In a medium bowl, mix flour, sugar, baking powder, and salt. Add melted butter and milk. Beat 2 minutes on high speed, or until mixture is smooth. Add egg and beat cake batter an additional 2 minutes.

In a heavy 10" skillet, melt butter over medium heat. Remove from heat and evenly distribute **Beth's Farm Kitchen Golden Pear Chutney** over melted butter. Gently pour cake batter over chutney in skillet. Be careful to maintain an even chutney distribution as you pour.

On a rack in center of oven, bake cake 40 - 45 minutes, or until golden in color and surface of cake springs back to the touch. Remove from oven and cool pan on wire rack for 5 minutes. With a spatula, loosen cake from skillet edge. Place serving platter over cake, and carefully turn skillet upside-down. Shake gently and lift off skillet. Top with almonds and serve with whipped cream.

Points of Interest about Pears

- Over-ripe Bartlett's are right for smoothies.

- Lemon juice will stop pears from browning.

- Harry & David™ made pears popular for Christmas.

- December is National Pear Month.

- Bartlett's and D'Anjou are the best poachers.

- The sweetness of pears complements spices.

- Use a melon baller to remove seeds, poach in white wine, and top with chutney.

- Grill pears with black pepper, and serve with pork cutlets.

- Use pears with pecorino cheese in risotto.

- Pears topped with a dollop of chutney and baked in the oven are delicious.

Chutney Triumphs

We have all had slip-ups in the kitchen. This recipe was one of those, and it made for a "teachable moment."

The tandoori chicken breast was marinated and ready for the grill ... then, 3 minutes on the grill, it was overcooked! What to do? **Beth's Farm Kitchen Golden Pear Chutney** to the rescue! Saved the meal!

....

No Oven Tonight

Sear 4 chicken cutlets. Drain. Add 1/2 cup **Beth's Farm Kitchen Golden Pear Chutney**. Heat through. Remove from heat. Add 1/2 cup plain yogurt drink.

Serve with cooked rice and sliced tomatoes.

Great summer, "I do not want to turn on the oven," dish.

Golden Braised Lamb

The flavors meld so well. Slow cooking really works in this easy recipe. Serve with broccoli over rice.

Makes 4 servings
Prep Time: 15 minutes   Cook Time: 6 - 8 hours

Ingredients
2 pounds cubed lamb or shanks
Sea salt and freshly ground black pepper
1/2 cup onions, chopped
1/2 cup red pepper, chopped
1 teaspoon olive oil
1/2 cup chicken stock
1/2 cup dry white wine
1 cup **Beth's Farm Kitchen Golden Pear Chutney**

Directions
Season meat with salt and pepper. Sauté meat, onions, and red pepper in oil. Add all ingredients to slow cooker and cook until tender according to manufacturer's directions. Another delish dish.

Chutneys 37

Beth's Farm Kitchen Hot Plum Chutney

This is a simple recipe with an elusive flavor. I am confident you are going to like it. This chutney has consistently been among our best-selling chutneys since my friend Grace passed it on to us many moons ago.

Makes 3 - 4 jars (8-ounce)
Prep Time: 35 minutes   Cook Time: 40 - 45 minutes

Ingredients
3 cups plums, pitted and halved (1 1/2 pounds pitted plums,
    2 pounds plums with pits)
1/2 cup light brown sugar
1/3 cup granulated sugar
1/2 cup cider vinegar
1 teaspoon red pepper flakes
1 teaspoon whole mustard seeds
1 clove garlic, chopped
1/4 medium onion, small dice
2 tablespoons crystallized ginger, chopped fine
3 tablespoons fresh ginger, chopped
1/2 cup golden raisins

Directions
Combine all ingredients in a medium saucepan. Cook over medium heat, stirring frequently, for 40 - 45 minutes, or until thickened. Take off heat and pour hot into sterilized jars or refrigerator containers.

Possibilities

Beth's Farm Kitchen Hot Plum Chutney can often be seen on event tables served with fine cheeses.

We love it with Old Chatham Sheepherding Company's award-winning Camembert.

It is also great in other ways:

- As a shrimp cocktail.
- In a baked Brie encroute.
- With cold noodles and sesame sauce.
- In cheese sandwiches.
- As a veggie burger topper.
- On savory crackers.
- In sage and plum pork chops.
- As a topping for salmon loaf or croquettes.
- Instead of marshmallows on sweet potato casserole.

Life in Jamland

One day, I tried to peel all of the season's peaches in one afternoon. We were awash in peach juice!

On more than one occasion, Charlie and I processed jars and cut plums way past midnight: brown hands, but lovely complexion!

Paula Deen was coming to tape a show: We painted the entire kitchen overnight in peach season, and then they filmed the show outside on the deck!

Japanese TV came to the kitchen; I was instructed to speak right into the camera. Of course, I was voiced over. The kitchen rocked the day we watched the program!

Elegantly Dressed Pork Tenderloin

Charlie and I spent the late 1970s reinventing Chinese food. What came out of all those cold noodles and "golden coins" was one incredible dish. We now put it together in minutes. We seldom purée the chutney, and it is always successful. One friend is positive I gave this to her as a lamb recipe, and it also works well in that interpretation.

Makes 4 - 6 servings
Prep Time: 15 minutes, plus 1- 8 hours for marinating
Cook Time: 20 minutes

Ingredients
For Marinade
1/2 cup **Beth's Farm Kitchen Hot Plum Chutney**
3 tablespoons soy sauce
3 tablespoons chunky peanut butter
2 tablespoons grated fresh ginger
1/4 cup dry red wine
2 tablespoons sesame oil or olive oil

For Pork
1 or 2 pork tenderloins
1/4 cup chopped cilantro or parsley (optional)

Directions
Mix marinade ingredients in a bowl and process with a stick blender or mini-chopper. Put marinade and meat in a freezer bag. Marinate in refrigerator for at least 1 hour, or up to 8 hours. Preheat oven to 400°F. Take meat out of refrigerator 1/2 hour before cooking. Lining pan with foil helps with clean-up. If cooking two tenderloins, separate them in dish for even cooking. Cook for 20 minutes. Remove meat from baking pan; let rest on a platter for 5 minutes. Slice meat and drizzle with sauce from pan. Garnish with cilantro or parsley. Serve with baked sweet potatoes, additional **Beth's Farm Kitchen Hot Plum Chutney**, and asparagus.

Beth's Farm Kitchen Cranberry-Lime Chutney

Quite zingy with no heat ... says it all. Try this in a pear, melon, and blueberry salad.

Makes 3 - 4 jars (8-ounce)
Prep Time: 25 minutes   Cook Time: 30 - 45 minutes

Ingredients
4 cups cranberries, rough-chopped in food processor
1/2 cup light brown sugar
1/2 orange (including rind), sliced thin
1/2 lime (including rind), sliced thin
1/2 cup cider vinegar
1/4 cup water
1/4 teaspoon ground nutmeg
1/4 teaspoon fresh grated ginger
1/4 teaspoon dry mustard
1/4 teaspoon ground allspice

Directions
Combine all ingredients in a medium saucepan. Cook over medium heat, stirring frequently, for 30 - 45 minutes, or until thickened. Take off heat and pour hot into sterilized jars or refrigerator containers.

Summer Salad

During the last two years, I have been noticing more chefs using watermelon. The best I have tasted is a watermelon, heirloom tomato, and blue cheese salad.

Beth's Farm Kitchen's riff on this is 1 cup watermelon, yellow or red, chunked, 1 large heirloom tomato, chopped, and 1 chopped peach.

The dressing is 1/2 cup **Beth's Farm Kitchen Cranberry-Lime Chutney**, slightly puréed, mixed with 1 tablespoon olive oil and 1/3 cup white balsamic vinegar.

Crumble blue cheese on top. I just love the taste!

Salmon with a Cranberry Slant

The vast majority of my friends and family grill. Here's their preferred variation on this recipe:

Use individual salmon steaks, one per person. Cook on a medium-hot grill for 5 - 6 minutes, until cooked halfway through. Turn fish, coat second side with chutney, and cook for 5 - 6 minutes, or until done.

This is my oven-baked method:

Preheat oven to 400°F. Lightly grease shallow baking pan with oil and place fish skin side down in pan. Add salt and pepper, to taste. Coat fish with **Beth's Farm Kitchen Chili Cranberry Chutney**. Bake in oven about 20 minutes. Serve with sautéed Swiss chard, mushrooms, and cherry tomatoes. Grilled or baked, the best!

Beth's Farm Kitchen Chili Cranberry Chutney

This chutney talks turkey to me. When served with sandwiches or hash, it gives just enough kick to lift your spirits. We have even topped off a carrot and parsnip mash with this chutney. Wow!

Makes 3 - 4 jars (8-ounce)
Prep Time: 15 minutes   Cook Time: 30 - 45 minutes

Ingredients
3 cups cranberries, rough-chopped in food processor
1/2 cup dark brown sugar
1/4 cup dark raisins
1/4 cup raspberry vinegar
1/2 apple, peeled, cored, small dice
1 tablespoon lemon juice
1/2 teaspoon fresh grated ginger
1 tablespoon red pepper flakes
1/2 teaspoon sambal oelek
1/4 teaspoon ground cinnamon
1/4 cup water

Directions
Combine all ingredients in a medium saucepan. Cook over medium heat, stirring frequently, for 30 - 45 minutes, or until thickened. Take off heat, and pour hot into sterilized jars or refrigerator containers.

Beth's Farm Kitchen Cranberry Horseradish Chutney

John and Patty from Hudson Valley Homestead gave this concept to Sacha Eaton of Beth's Farm Kitchen to develop. Since we all liked it, they suggested we use it, and, as they say, the rest is history.

Makes 3 - 4 jars (8-ounce)
Prep Time: 10 minutes   Cook Time: 15 minutes

Ingredients
1/4 cup orange juice
1/4 cup wasabi powder
5 cups cranberries, rough-chopped in food processor
3/4 cup light brown sugar
1 cup fresh horseradish, ground
1/4 cup prepared mustard

Directions
Combine orange juice and wasabi powder in a bowl and set aside. Combine cranberries, sugar, horseradish and mustard in a medium saucepan. Bring to a boil over high heat and immediately remove. Add mixture of orange juice and wasabi powder, stir, and pour hot into sterilized jars or refrigerator containers.

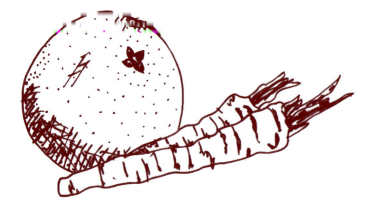

Cran-Horse at Your Service

- With oysters.
- On brisket.
- With lox and bagels.
- As a tuna burger topper.
- In deviled eggs.
- With cheddar cheese.
- Added to chicken salad.
- As a kielbasa sausage dip.

A Smattering of History

The lure of the Spice Islands influenced the histories of Greece, Persia, Portugal, Spain, Holland, England and Italy. Through my reading, I followed the spice trail history from China (soy ketsup), through Mongolia (hot pots) and northern India (wheat), and southward to Malaysia (nutmeg, cinnamon, cardamom and turmeric). The seafaring nations were probing the coasts and islands, while landlubbers were descending from the north. The stories are brutal, and it was all for profit. Nothing changes.

Classic Monte Cristo Sandwich with Horseradish Twist

This is a dressed-up version of the classic grilled cheese. I have found that half a sandwich is enough for me, unless chopping wood was a part of the day's activities. A fresh fruit salad with mint is a refreshing accompaniment.

Makes 6 servings
Prep Time: 20 minutes   Cook Time: 10 minutes

Ingredients
1 pound loaf crusty bread
1 cup **Beth's Farm Kitchen Cranberry Horseradish Chutney**
12 slices cheese, such as Gruyère, horseradish cheddar, or Havarti dill
6 slices smoked duck
6 slices ham, baked, boiled or smoked
4 large eggs
1/4 cup heavy cream
3 tablespoons butter

Directions
Cut bread into 12 equal slices. Spread **Beth's Farm Kitchen Cranberry Horseradish Chutney** on six slices. Layer cheese, duck, ham, and again cheese on six slices. Top with six other slices of bread. Close each sandwich firmly to seal. In a medium bowl, whisk eggs and cream. Dip each sandwich in egg batter, allowing excess to fall back into bowl.

Preheat a heavy-gauge griddle or frying pan over medium heat. Melt butter on griddle, but do not allow it to brown. Arrange sandwiches on griddle and cook about 3 minutes per side, until egg batter is golden brown and cheese is melted. Serve hot.

Beth's Farm Kitchen Madras Nectar Chutney

This chutney has a long history. It took us a while to perfect the combination of toasted spices and nectarines. We have so much to learn from the cooking techniques of India. The subtleties are tricky.

Makes 3 - 4 jars (8-ounce)
Prep Time: 35 minutes
Cook Time: 30 - 45 minutes

Ingredients

3 cups nectarines, pitted and sliced
1/2 clove garlic, chopped
1/2 medium onion, small dice
1 tablespoon hot red cherry pepper, chopped
1/4 cup light brown sugar
2 tablespoons orange juice
2 tablespoons cider vinegar
1 teaspoon fresh ginger, chopped
1 teaspoon curry powder
1/3 orange (including rind), sliced thin
1/3 lemon (including rind), sliced thin
1/2 teaspoon garam masala
2 tablespoons sliced almonds

Directions

Combine all ingredients, except almonds, in a medium saucepan. Cook over medium heat, stirring frequently, for 30 - 45 minutes, or until thickened. Remove from heat, stir in almonds, and pour hot into sterilized jars or refrigerator containers.

History Lesson Continued

The traditional vegetarian diet of India absorbed flavors and products from its invaders. The Moghuls (Persians) brought rice and meats. The Chinese brought sweets and stir-fry. The Portuguese brought tomatoes, potatoes and chilies from countries they had conquered. The British brought a unifying language and made tea the drink of India. Arab trading networks transported these foods across the subcontinent for all to taste.

Chutney, whether fresh, sweet, or any other style, was the unifying condiment on every table.

Chutney is Global

Since 300 BC, wars have been fought, empires have blossomed and died, and thousands of ships and sailors have been destroyed in pursuit of the spices in chutney.

Wherever global traders and conquerors traveled, by camel or ship, food was scarce. Available were dry and flavorless hardtack biscuits, a mixture of flour and water baked to remove all moisture. There was a need for a condiment that could be sweet, sour, or salty. Chutney filled the bill. Sugar, vinegar, and salt are preservatives that make condiments stable, tasty, and edible for months without refrigeration.

Do you think the term "good for the long haul" refers to chutney?

Carrot Nectar Soup

This soup is a beautiful color; I serve it in red glass bowls. Generally, I consider this a fall soup, because the carrots are sweeter in autumn, but it is equally good chilled on a summer night. We have substituted winter squash for the carrots. So it is a soup for all seasons, and it adapts well to tweaking.

Makes 4 - 6 servings
Prep Time: 20 minutes   Cook Time: 30 - 40 minutes

Ingredients
1 pound carrots, peeled and small dice
2 tablespoons uncooked rice*
8 cups water
1/2 cup **Beth's Farm Kitchen Madras Nectar Chutney**
1 cup light cream (optional)
Sea salt and freshly ground black pepper, to taste
Chopped red peppers, for garnish

Directions
Simmer carrots, rice, and water in a pot until carrots are tender (20 - 30 minutes). Purée while adding **Beth's Farm Kitchen Madras Nectar Chutney**. Return to pot, add cream (optional), and season, and warm through. Garnish with peppers.

* The rice adds a silky smoothness to the soup when puréed.

Chutneys

Beth's Farm Kitchen Peach Chutney

Makes 3 - 4 jars (8-ounce)
Prep Time: 45 minutes   Cook Time: 30 - 45 minutes

Ingredients
4 cups peaches, peeled, pitted and sliced
1/2 medium onion, small dice
1 clove garlic, chopped
2 tablespoons fresh chopped ginger
1 cup light brown sugar
1/2 cup granulated sugar
3/4 cup cider vinegar
2 teaspoons whole mustard seeds
1 teaspoon ground cinnamon
1/2 teaspoon ground allspice
1 teaspoon red pepper flakes
2 tablespoons golden raisins
2 tablespoons dried currants

Directions
Combine all ingredients in a medium saucepan. Cook over medium heat, stirring frequently, for 30 - 45 minutes, or until thickened. Take off heat and pour hot into sterilized jars or refrigerator containers.

The Tale of Roti and Chutney

I met Susie and Emory Sanders in Tortola for three days of sailing. The first day, just to get acclimated, we went ashore for a roti lunch.

We were the only people at this eatery, so we started talking to the server and she invited us back to the kitchen to see the roti made. (A roti is a cross between a crêpe and a tortilla.)

A wonderful woman from Nevis was flipping the roti as if they were pancakes, and stirring a big pot of mango chutney. It looked like my chunky **Beth's Farm Kitchen Peach Chutney**, and she was almost ready to put it in a blender, because, in Tortola, they like their chutney smooth. She gave us a taste; it was musky, with medium heat. A great experience for this chutney-maker!

Tamale Treats

We will never compete with the Tamale Lady at the Greenmarket, but these make a great snack.

Ingredients
2 pounds braised and shredded pork butt
1 cup **Beth's Farm Kitchen Bellow Yellow Chutney**
1 package dried cornhusks (soaked in warm water for 20 minutes)
1 prepared mix recipe masa harina

Directions
Mix meat and chutney. Set aside. Lay out cornhusks. Spread 1 tablespoon prepared masa on each husk, and place 1 tablespoon mixture of meat and chutney in center. Fold each husk to form a parcel and tie with a strip of cornhusk. Steam parcels for 1 hour in stockpot with a few inches of boiling water. Check water level in steamer pot to prevent burning. Remove from steamer. Serve hot with salad or freeze for another day.

Grilled Cheese and Chutney Sandwich

Makes 6 servings
Prep Time: 5 minutes   *Cook Time: 10 minutes*

Ingredients
For Sandwich
6 crusty sandwich rolls
1 cup **Beth's Farm Kitchen Peach Chutney**
3 tablespoons tangy mustard
8 ounces Gruyère cheese, grated
1 1/2 cups baby arugula or watercress
4 ounces St. André cheese, rind trimmed, and sliced
2 tablespoons olive oil

For Salsa
1 cup **Beth's Farm Kitchen Spicy Corn Relish**
1 can (15 1/2-ounce) black beans, rinsed and drained
1 scallion, sliced thin
1 tomato, seeded and chopped
2 tablespoons cumin
2 tablespoons chopped jalapeño
Olive oil

Directions
Slice and toast rolls. Spread **Beth's Farm Kitchen Peach Chutney** on one side of each roll and mustard on other side. Layer mustard sides with Gruyère, arugula, St. André, and finally more Gruyère. Close rolls. Brush outside of rolls lightly with oil. Grill in fry pan, pressing down firmly before turning over. Continue grilling until sandwiches are golden brown and cheese is melted. Combine salsa ingredients and serve on side. Great Saturday lunch.

Chutneys 47

New-Style Roasted Vegetables with Cilantro Yogurt Sauce

Makes 4 - 6 servings
Prep Time: 30 minutes   Cook Time: 30 - 60 minutes

Ingredients
For Vegetables
4 small zucchini
4 small eggplants
3 peppers, mixture of red, yellow and green
2 sweet onions
6 plum tomatoes
3 jalapeño peppers, or more to taste
Olive oil
Sea salt
1/2 cup **Beth's Farm Kitchen Peach Chutney**

For Sauce
3 cups chopped cilantro
1 tablespoon fresh lime juice
1 cup plain yogurt
1 cup sour cream

Directions
For Vegetables
Preheat oven to 375°F. Cut vegetables into 1/2"-thick slices and toss in olive oil. Spread evenly on two 11" x 13" baking sheets. Sprinkle with salt. Bake for up to 1 hour, turning once so they brown evenly. When roasting is almost done, top with **Beth's Farm Kitchen Peach Chutney** and cook for last 10 minutes. Watch that vegetables do not burn. Tomatoes and jalapeños cook quickly, and peppers and onions can take up to 1 hour. Remove vegetables as they are done and put on serving platter.

For Sauce
While vegetables are roasting, make sauce. Combine ingredients, whisk lightly, and chill. The sauce really makes dish, so do not skip. Serve vegetables at room temperature over rice, topped with sauce. Make this a year-round dish by choosing vegetables that are in season. For instance, in winter, slow roast carrots, parsnips, turnips and potatoes.

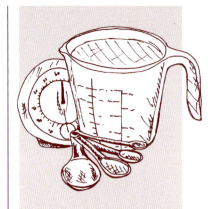

Early Job Security

The first job I had was as a short-order cook at a hospital coffee shop, when I was 16, and I had some adventures there!

The doctor who ordered poached eggs every Saturday morning was a saint; he never complained about his "yokes on toast."

I just did not have the knack or timing for swirling the vinegar-saturated water. I have improved, though. Now, I use poached-egg cups. Wisdom and age!

Saucy 'n' Savory

During the winter, we return home from markets chilled to the bone, and we want to eat instantly. Warm and hardy, this is the dish for those moments.

Makes 4 servings
Prep Time: 20 minutes
Cook Time: 20 minutes

Cook 1 1/2 cups red potatoes, medium chop. Parboil 4 sausages in water or beer. Cool. Remove casings. Chop sausages, and set aside. Sauté together 1/2 cup diced red pepper, 1 sliced onion, 6 sliced mushrooms, and 1/2 cup frozen corn. Add potatoes, sausages, 1/2 cup **Beth's Farm Kitchen Hot 'n' Spicy Chutney**, and 1/2 bottle (12-ounce) beer. Season with salt and pepper. Heat through while stirring. Serve in bowls.

Beth's Farm Kitchen Hot 'n' Spicy Chutney

One of our customers buys this chutney for his annual tourtière. It is a traditional French Canadian holiday pie resembling shepherd's pie.

Makes 3 - 4 jars (8-ounce)
Prep Time: 35 minutes   *Cook Time: 30 - 45 minutes*

Ingredients
2 or 3 apples, peeled, cored, and small dice
3/4 cup dark raisins
1/2 medium onion, small dice
1/4 cup red bell pepper, medium dice
1/4 cup green bell pepper, medium dice
1 cup dark brown sugar
1/2 cup cider vinegar
2 tablespoons whole mustard seeds
3/4 teaspoon red pepper flakes
3/4 teaspoon ground cayenne
1 1/2 teaspoons chopped jalapeño peppers
1/2 chopped clove garlic
1 teaspoon chopped fresh ginger

Directions
Combine all ingredients in a medium saucepan. Cook over medium heat, stirring frequently, for 30 - 45 minutes, or until thickened. Take off heat and pour hot into sterilized jars or refrigerator containers.

Chutneys   49

Beth's Farm Kitchen Delta Road Chutney

Delta Road brings to mind smooth and mellow, as in "down on the delta," and I often think of Helen Reddy's rather sultry version of "Delta Dawn." This chutney also reminds me of Christmas. See the following page for a recipe using **Beth's Farm Kitchen Delta Road Chutney**.

Makes 3 - 4 jars (8-ounce)
Prep Time: 35 minutes   Cook Time: 30 - 45 minutes

Ingredients

1 1/3 cups peaches, peeled, pitted, and sliced
1 apple, peeled, cored, and small dice
1/2 cup dark raisins
1/4 orange, sliced thin (including rind)
1/2 medium onion, small dice
1/4 cup red bell pepper, small dice
1/4 cup green bell pepper, small dice
3/4 cup light brown sugar
1/4 cup cider vinegar
1 chopped clove garlic
1 tablespoon chopped fresh ginger
1/4 teaspoon ground cinnamon
2 tablespoons whole mustard seeds
2 teaspoons ground allspice
1/2 teaspoon ground clove
1/2 teaspoon ground nutmeg

Directions

Combine all ingredients in a medium saucepan. Cook over medium heat, stirring frequently, for 30 - 45 minutes, or until thickened. Take off heat and pour hot into sterilized jars or refrigerator containers.

Life is Easier with Chutney

Makes 4 - 6 servings
Prep Time: 15 minutes
Cook Time: 20 minutes

Ingredients

4 boneless chicken breasts*
1/2 cup mayonnaise
1 cup plain yogurt
1 cup chopped celery
1/2 cup chopped scallions
1/2 cup **Beth's Farm Kitchen Rhubarb Chutney**
Sea salt and pepper
1/2 cup chopped walnuts (optional)

Directions

Cut chicken into bite-size pieces. Combine remaining ingredients and add chicken. Serve on a hard roll or a bed of greens. Simply delicious!

* Buy roasted chicken breasts or deli rotisserie chicken. Make it easy for yourself, especially in summer. Less is better.

Salad-Green Amounts

Salad greens are not just head lettuces anymore. There is now a wide variety of leaf lettuces to choose from. How do we measure our greens?

For **head lettuces**, which include Iceberg, Romaine, Boston and Bibb, 1 ounce is equivalent to 1 cup.

For **leaf lettuces**, including baby spinach, arugula and mesclun, 1 ounce is equivalent to 1 1/2 cups. When recipe directions call for "lightly packed," drop leaves into a measuring cup and press them down lightly with fingers.

Grilled Peach and Chutney Salad

This recipe was given to us by the chefs at Great Performances, a catering and event-planning company in New York City. They run Katchkie Farm in Kinderhook, New York, an organic farm that educates inner-city kids about farming and healthy eating through the Sylvia Foundation. Beth's Farm Kitchen worked on developing their tomato sauce and ketsup recipes. The chefs' take on **Beth's Farm Kitchen Delta Road Chutney** has turned me around from all winter to all seasons for this chutney.

Makes 4 - 6 servings
Prep Time: 15 minutes   Cook Time: 6 minutes

Ingredients
1 cup **Beth's Farm Kitchen Delta Road Chutney**
1 jalapeño, sliced into rounds and soaked in cold water for 10 minutes
1 small red onion, small dice
1/2 cup minced cilantro
1 tablespoon olive oil
5 - 6 peaches cut into eighths
8 - 10 ounces baby arugula or baby spinach
1/2 cup crumbled blue cheese

Directions
Prepare grill for cooking over medium coals. In a bowl, mix **Beth's Farm Kitchen Delta Road Chutney**, jalapeño, onion, cilantro and oil. Set aside. Toss peaches in oil, and cook until slightly charred and showing grill marks, about 3 minutes per side. Remove from grill and put directly into chutney mixture, carefully turning warm peaches to coat all sides. Add peach and chutney mixture to arugula or spinach and fold in blue cheese. Serve with grilled hot dogs or bratwurst and breadsticks. Simple and sublime.

Sweet, Sweet Potato Salad

We look at sweet potatoes only in the fall, but they should become your favorites year-round. Here's why: They have more fiber than a bowl of oatmeal, more potassium than a banana, and lots of vitamin C. This is an adaptation of a recipe by Monica Bhide that appeared in the November/December 2010 issue of *AARP* magazine.

Makes 6 servings
Prep Time: 20 minutes   Cook Time: 20 minutes

Ingredients
For Salad
1/4 cup olive oil
3 large sweet potatoes, peeled, and small dice
1 sprig fresh rosemary, chopped
Sea salt and freshly ground black pepper
1/2 teaspoon cumin
1 teaspoon fresh grated ginger
1 cup sliced almonds, toasted
1 cup scallions, chopped
1 cup julienned roasted red peppers

For Dressing
6 tablespoons white wine vinegar
1/3 cup **Beth's Farm Kitchen Delta Road Chutney**
2 tablespoons Dijon mustard
1/4 cup olive oil

Directions
Preheat oven to 350°F. Drizzle oil over sweet potatoes and roast until cooked. While potatoes are roasting, make dressing by whisking vinegar, chutney and mustard in bowl; slowly add oil, whisking continuously. Put potatoes in a bowl and add remaining salad ingredients, plus dressing. Toss and serve.

Mom and Antoinette

As kids, none of the seven Linskey children thought of Mom as a good cook.

The Cream of Wheat always had lumps, and the Spam™ was sometimes overcooked.

My older sister was sure Mom just didn't have the time to learn to cook.

Seven kids did keep Mom busy. We all went to Catholic school, which meant we needed fresh white blouses and shirts everyday. In those days, there was no such thing as "easy-care cotton." So, while we were in school, Mom ironed all day in front of the TV. She even had a mangle!

I don't think Mom lacked interest in cooking, though.

While ironing those mountains of blouses and shirts, she watched Antoinette and François Pope on their TV show, "Creative Cookery."

Mom also had the Antoinette Pope cookbook. My older sister Rita Ann, its current owner, says the book was already held together by red tape when Mom gave it to her.

Mom may even have taken classes from the Popes. Their classes cost only $1 each in 1936, when she was still single and working in downtown Chicago.

Beth's Farm Kitchen Green Tomato Chutney

When faced with unripe green tomatoes, many cooks reach for the deep fryer, as in that very poignant, hilariously funny film, "Fried Green Tomatoes." Reach for the saucepot instead and whip up this chutney. You can freeze green tomatoes in season in batches, and this chutney can be made all year.

Makes 3 - 4 jars (8-ounce)
Prep Time: 35 minutes   Cook Time: 30 - 45 minutes

Ingredients
3 1/3 cups green tomatoes, seeded, medium dice
1/3 lemon (including rind), sliced thin
1/3 orange (including rind), sliced thin
1 clove garlic, chopped
1/4 cup chopped fresh ginger
1 teaspoon dry mustard
1/3 teaspoon ground allspice
1/2 teaspoon ground cayenne
1/2 teaspoon tamarind paste
1/3 cup cider vinegar
1 cup light brown sugar
1 medium onion, small dice
1 teaspoon hot red cherry pepper, chopped
2 tablespoons golden raisins
2 tablespoons dark raisins
1/2 teaspoon sambal oelek
1/4 cup sliced almonds

Directions
Combine all ingredients, except almonds, in a medium saucepan. Cook over medium heat, stirring frequently, for 30 - 45 minutes, or until thickened. Take off heat, stir in almonds, and pour hot into sterilized jars or refrigerator containers.

Chutneys   53

Vegetable Turnover: The Best New Snack Food

These are wonderful to have tucked away in your freezer for when company pops in. They are satisfying and, served with a salad, make a quick and pretty meal. Beats take-out pizza!

Makes 6 servings
Prep Time: 30 minutes   Cook Time: 1 hour

Ingredients
3 medium carrots, small dice
1 large sweet potato, small dice
1 medium baking potato, small dice
2 cloves garlic, minced
3 tablespoons olive oil
1 tablespoon fresh rosemary, thyme, or basil, chopped
Sea salt and freshly ground black pepper
1 cup **Beth's Farm Kitchen Green Tomato Chutney**
1 container freezer pie crust dough or your homemade recipe (see sidebar)

Directions
Preheat oven to 425°F. Toss vegetables with oil, rosemary, salt and pepper. Spread vegetables in one layer on large baking pan. Bake for 20 - 25 minutes, until vegetables are tender. Remove from oven and place in large bowl. Add **Beth's Farm Kitchen Green Tomato Chutney** and mix. Lower oven temperature to 375°F. Roll out dough and cut into 6 squares. Put vegetables on dough and fold to form turnovers. Press edges of dough with fork to seal. Place turnovers on baking sheet and bake at 375°F for 15 - 20 minutes, or until crust is golden. Serve either hot or at room temperature. A healthy, tasty afternoon snack.

Your Own Dough

If you would like to make your own dough for the vegetable turnover recipe, we recommend that you make turnover-crust dough. Here's how:

Ingredients
2 cups all-purpose flour
1/2 cup canola oil
1/3 cup milk
1/2 teaspoon salt

Directions
Mix ingredients with a fork until they hold together. Form into a flattened ball. Wrap in waxed paper. Chill for 1/2 hour. Roll out between 2 pieces of waxed paper. Cut into 6 squares, fill, fold, crimp, bake and eat.

Note: Do not feel guilty about buying a premade crust or pizza dough!

Sauce Notes

Ragin' Rémoulade (Page 57)

1/4 cup **Beth's Farm Kitchen Ragin' Rhubarb Chutney**, 1/4 cup mayonnaise, 2 tablespoons whole grain mustard, 2 tablespoons chopped fresh dill. Serve as a spread for buttermilk biscuits or as a condiment for grilled leg of lamb.

Corn and Black Bean Salsa (Page 47)

1 cup **Beth's Farm Kitchen Spicy Corn Relish**, 1 can (15 1/2-ounce) black beans, rinsed and drained, 1 scallion, sliced thin, 1 tomato, seeded and chopped, 2 tablespoons cumin, 2 tablespoons chopped jalapeño and olive oil. Tortilla chips are perfect with this.

Cilantro Sauce (Page 48)

3 cups cilantro, chopped, 1 tablespoon fresh lime juice, 1 cup plain yogurt, 1 cup sour cream. This sauce is good with vegetable fritters or potato pancakes.

Chicken Tenders: Sauced and Served

This dipping sauce goes very well with chicken tenders. It can also be used with grilled fish or as a salad dressing, so make extra.

Makes 4 - 6 servings as appetizer
Prep Time: 20 minutes, plus 2 - 4 hours for marinating
Cook Time: 10 minutes

Ingredients
For Chicken
2 eggs
3/4 cup puréed **Beth's Farm Kitchen Green Tomato Chutney**
1 tablespoon soy sauce
1 pound chicken tenders
2 cups dried bread crumbs
Sea salt and freshly ground pepper
1/4 cup chopped parsley

For Dipping Sauce
1 cup **Beth's Farm Kitchen Rhubarb Chutney**, puréed
1/2 cup yogurt

Directions
For Chicken
Preheat oven to 350°F. Beat eggs, 1/2 cup **Beth's Farm Kitchen Green Tomato Chutney**, and soy sauce together. Place chicken in mix, cover, and marinate in refrigerator for 2 - 4 hours. When ready to cook, mix bread crumbs, salt and pepper, parsley, and 1/4 cup **Beth's Farm Kitchen Green Tomato Chutney** in another bowl. Chutney gives breading a large-crumb texture. Remove chicken from marinade and dip tenders in crumb mixture. Carefully place chicken on a cookie sheet and bake for 10 minutes. Remove when they are lightly browned. You can pan fry, if you prefer.

For Dipping Sauce
Combine **Beth's Farm Kitchen Rhubarb Chutney** and yogurt in food processor for a quick spin. Chicken tenders love this coating.

Chutneys   55

Beth's Farm Kitchen Ragin' Rhubarb Chutney and Beth's Farm Kitchen Rhubarb Chutney

The difference between these two rhubarb chutneys is the peppers we use in each. **Beth's Farm Kitchen Ragin' Rhubarb Chutney** uses habanero peppers, and **Beth's Farm Kitchen Rhubarb Chutney** uses round hot red cherry peppers. Truth be told, we make these two very similar chutneys because one day there was trouble in the kitchen with "pepper identification." The orange habaneros were mistaken for the hot red cherry peppers. Fortunately, the error was caught in the kitchen. We liked the taste and decided to sell it. Public opinion told us to keep making it.

Makes 3 - 4 jars (8-ounce)
Prep Time: 45 minutes   Cook Time: 30 - 45 minutes

Ingredients
4 cups rhubarb, large dice
1 cup light brown sugar
1 cup cider vinegar
1 medium onion, sliced thin
2 tablespoons fresh chopped ginger
1/4 cup dark raisins
1 hot red cherry pepper, chopped (**Beth's Farm Kitchen Ragin' Rhubarb Chutney**: Use 1/2 habanero pepper, chopped)
2 teaspoons tamarind paste
2 teaspoons whole mustard seeds
1/2 teaspoon ground fenugreek
1/2 teaspoon pickling spices (placed in a spice bag)
1 or 2 apples, peeled, cored, and small dice

Directions
Combine ingredients in a medium saucepan. Cook over medium heat, stirring frequently, for 30 - 45 minutes, or until thickened. Take off heat, remove spice bag, and pour hot into sterilized jars or refrigerator containers.

Sauces and Chutney

The dipping sauce for the chicken tenders (on Page 55) is an example of how chutneys are used in parts of India and in many Indian homes in the United States. Tartar sauce is just about the same thing, from English-speaking countries.

Mix the chutney with yogurt and blend in a food processor and use for vegetables, chicken fingers, grilled fish, even a dressing for a salad.

Try doubling the recipe for the rémoulade (on Page 57) to have it ready for another day's use, just as Indian cooks do with their chutneys.

Veggie Salad à la Beth's

Makes 4 - 6 servings
Prep Time: 30 minutes
Cook Time: none

Ingredients
3 carrots
2 apples
2 white turnips
1 bunch radishes
2 scallions, sliced thin
1 bunch fresh cilantro, chopped
1 cup **Beth's Farm Kitchen Rhubarb Chutney**

Directions
Shred all vegetables, except cilantro, in a food processor. Squeeze out some juice (which, by the way, makes a tasty veggie drink). Chill vegetables. Toss with cilantro and **Beth's Farm Kitchen Rhubarb Chutney**. Serve.

This is great on a pulled-pork sandwich, as a po' boy, as an hors d'oeuvre rolled in a lettuce leaf, or as a side salad. Adjust vegetables to your taste and the season.

Ragin' Cajun Shrimp Po' Boy

This is so good, you will want two. No joke!

Makes 4 servings
Prep Time: 20 minutes   Cook Time: 15 minutes

Ingredients
For Shrimp
3/4 pound raw, peeled, and deveined shrimp
Sea salt and freshly ground black pepper
1 egg, whisked
1 cup bread crumbs (traditional or Japanese-style)
Vegetable oil, for pan-frying
4 crusty rolls
1 head lettuce, Boston or Bibb

For Rémoulade
1/4 cup **Beth's Farm Kitchen Ragin' Rhubarb Chutney**
1/4 cup mayonnaise
2 tablespoons whole grain mustard
2 tablespoons chopped fresh dill

Directions
Mix ingredients for rémoulade and set aside. Season shrimp with salt and pepper. Dip shrimp in egg and then bread crumbs. Heat oil in heavy fry pan and quickly stir-fry breaded shrimp until they are golden and begin to curl. Slice rolls in half, layer lettuce onto bread, and add shrimp. Drizzle sandwich lightly with rémoulade. Serve hot.

Chutneys

Goat Cheese and Greens Pizza

Using your own dough or a prepared crust, cook this pizza on the grill or in the oven. Spinach, arugula, and Swiss chard are all winners! There are so many possible variations. You can add mushrooms, change the chutney or the cheese, or use tomato sauce.

Makes 4 - 6 appetizer servings, 2 or 3 lunch servings
Prep Time: 20 minutes   Cook Time: 15 - 20 minutes

Ingredients
Pizza dough or a prepared crust
Olive oil
4 cups fresh baby spinach, arugula, or Swiss chard
2 tablespoons **Beth's Farm Kitchen Garlic Jelly**
1 cup **Beth's Farm Kitchen Ragin' Rhubarb Chutney**
2-ounce button fresh goat cheese, without rind
3 tablespoons grated parmesan cheese
Sea salt and freshly ground black pepper

Directions
Preheat oven to 425°F. Stretch dough to fit pizza pan, or use prepared crust. Brush olive oil over top of dough and set aside.

Sauté greens briefly with **Beth's Farm Kitchen Garlic Jelly** until leaves wilt. Set aside. Purée 1/2 cup of **Beth's Farm Kitchen Ragin' Rhubarb Chutney** and spread over pizza dough or prepared crust. Layer greens over chutney and crumble goat cheese on top of greens. Spread remaining chutney in dollops. Sprinkle parmesan; season with salt and pepper. Bake for 15 - 20 minutes, or until bottom of pizza is golden brown.

Dazzling Dip

Holiday parties are great fun, but the fare is usually pretty standard. This dip will make a statement.

Ingredients
1 avocado, mashed
1 cup **Beth's Farm Kitchen Cranberry Horseradish Chutney**
1/2 cup **Beth's Farm Kitchen Cranberry Sauce**

Directions
Mix ingredients. Place in a serving bowl and surround with carrot sticks, steamed broccoli florets, and jicama sticks.

How to Make a Samosa

Here is our easy take on a samosa:

Brush a flour tortilla with an egg wash. Place a heaping tablespoon of dal in the center, then fold and roll. Place it on a hot oiled fry pan, put a weight on tortilla, and cook one side until golden. Turn over and brown, and you are done. Your very own quick street food for lunch. Don't forget the extra helping of chutney!

Don's Dal

This dal is a standard in a samosa at the Wild Hive Farm Bakery. Don Lewis shared his recipe with us, and we have stayed fairly true to the original. But if you are up in Clinton Corners, New York, I strongly recommend the real thing.

Makes 4 - 5 servings
Prep Time: 30 minutes   *Cook Time: 40 minutes*

Ingredients
1 medium onion, small dice
1 cup canned garbanzo beans, drained
2 or 3 cloves garlic, small dice
Olive oil
1 1/2 cups finely sliced cabbage
1 tablespoon grated fresh ginger
1 sweet red pepper, small dice
2 tablespoons curry powder
2 cups warm water or vegetable stock
1 cup lentils
1 cup potatoes, medium dice
1/2 cup **Beth's Farm Kitchen Hot Plum Chutney**
1 teaspoon salt
1/2 cup chopped cilantro

Directions
Sauté onion, beans and garlic in oil until golden brown. Add cabbage, ginger, pepper, and curry powder. Deglaze pan with water or stock. Add lentils and potatoes and simmer for about 25 minutes. The finished consistency should be like that of mashed potatoes. If too thick, add more water or stock. Mix in chutney, add salt to taste, and fold in cilantro. Serve with a generous helping of **Beth's Farm Kitchen Hot Plum Chutney** as a side dish. Or make our multicultural samosa (see sidebar).

Chutneys   59

Beth's Farm Kitchen Bellow Yellow Chutney

Makes 3 - 4 jars (8-ounce)
Prep Time: 45 minutes   Cook Time: 30 - 45 minutes

Ingredients

4 cups yellow tomatoes (seeded and chopped medium) or
    small yellow cherry tomatoes (whole)
1/2 cup red pepper, small dice
1/2 cup yellow pepper, small dice
1/2 habanero pepper, chopped
1/2 cup granulated sugar
1/2 clove garlic, chopped
3 tablespoons fresh ginger, chopped
1 medium onion, small dice
1/2 cup white vinegar
1/4 teaspoon ground cloves
1/4 teaspoon ground cayenne
1 teaspoon sambal oelek
1/2 teaspoon whole mustard seeds
1 teaspoon red pepper flakes
2 tablespoons dried currants
2 tablespoons chopped walnuts

Directions

Add all ingredients, except walnuts, into a medium
saucepan. Cook over medium heat, stirring frequently, for
30 - 45 minutes, or until thickened. Stir in walnuts. Pour hot
into sterilized jars or refrigerator containers.

A Life of Spice

Someone sent me the link to NPR's "Kitchen Window," by Monica Bhide, in April 2009. Since then, her book "A Life of Spice" has been a great resource. Her web site is www.monicabhide.com. I asked Monica if I could use her recipe as an example of a fresh chutney, and her answer was "yes."

This chutney is made daily and used within 2 or 3 days in many Indian homes. Beth's Farm Kitchen's chutneys are made with sugar and vinegar, and cooked and canned. They have a long shelf life.

Mint-Cilantro Chutney from Monica Bhide

Makes 1 cup

Ingredients
- 1 cup packed chopped cilantro (leaves and stems)
- 1 cup packed mint (leaves only)
- 1 green serrano chili (remove seeds for less heat)
- 1/4 small red onion, sliced
- 2 tablespoons fresh lemon juice
- 1/2 teaspoon salt
- Up to 2 tablespoons water

Directions
Blend cilantro, mint, chili, onion, lemon juice, and salt into a smooth paste. To aid blending, add water. Chill and serve.

Small variations include roasted peanuts for texture and yogurt for creaminess. This chutney can be used as a spread on bread, as a salad dressing, or as a sauce on chicken. It can be refrigerated for 2 - 3 days.

Broccoli Rabe and Chutney Dance the Couscous Together

Makes 4 - 6 servings
Prep Time: 10 minutes   Cook Time: 25 minutes

Ingredients
- 2 1/2 cups water
- 1 1/2 cups Israeli couscous
- 1/2 cup **Beth's Farm Kitchen Bellow Yellow Chutney**
- 1 teaspoon olive oil
- 1 bunch broccoli rabe, washed, drained, and finely chopped*
- 1/2 - 1 cup vegetable broth or chicken stock

Directions
Bring water to a boil in a medium pot; stir in couscous and **Beth's Farm Kitchen Bellow Yellow Chutney**. Reduce heat and simmer until liquid has mostly evaporated and couscous is tender, about 15 - 20 minutes.

As couscous cooks, sauté broccoli rabe with oil for 2 minutes. Add up to 1 cup broth or stock to sauté pan, bring to a boil, cover, and cook for about 5 minutes, until rabe is tender. Drain.

When couscous is ready, transfer to a bowl and stir in broccoli rabe.

* Bok choy and Swiss chard work just as well.

Beth's Farm Kitchen Zapricot Chutney

The "Zap" in "Zapricot" comes from the chipotle peppers. They add a smoky heat.

Makes 3 - 4 jars (8-ounce)
Prep Time: 35 minutes   Cook Time: 30 - 45 minutes

Ingredients
3 cups apricots, pitted and halved
1/2 cup light brown sugar
1/3 cup cider vinegar
2 tablespoons dried currants
1/2 medium onion, small dice
1/2 teaspoon fresh grated ginger
1/2 teaspoon whole mustard seeds
1/2 teaspoon ground allspice
1/2 teaspoon tamarind paste
1/2 teaspoon ground chipotle
1 clove garlic, chopped
1/3 lime (including rind), sliced thin
2 tablespoons chopped walnuts

Directions
Combine all ingredients, except walnuts, in a medium saucepan. Cook over medium heat, stirring frequently, for 30 - 45 minutes, or until thickened. Take off heat, stir in walnuts, and pour hot into sterilized jars or refrigerator containers.

Potato and Sausage Salad

Makes 6 servings
(1/2 cup per person)
Prep Time: 45 minutes
Cook Time: 20 minutes

Ingredients
3 cups Quattro's smoked pheasant sausage, medium dice
3 cups new red potatoes, skins on, cooked, medium dice
1/2 cup green beans, blanched and chopped
1/4 medium onion, small dice
6 **Beth's Farm Kitchen Dilly Beans**, small dice
1/2 cup chopped parsley
1 cup **Beth's Farm Kitchen Zapricot Chutney**

Directions
Combine all ingredients and toss lightly. Chill for several hours and serve.

Dining with Doris

Doris Jackson, a dear friend, loves the finer things in life, and pâté is one of her weaknesses.

To her, Prosecco and pâté are a proper dinner. Our friends at Hudson Valley Duck Farm in the Greenmarket have the answer. Whenever we plan a special evening for Doris, I order their pâté. Local and luscious.

Serve pâté, **Beth's Farm Kitchen Zapricot Chutney**, and French bread. Pour the chilled Prosecco and enjoy the evening.

Beth's Farm Kitchen Quincherry Chutney

We used this chutney in a duck sauce in the jam chapter, Page 19. We recommend serving this with manchego cheese as a quince paste substitute.

Makes 5 jars (8-ounce)
Prep Time: 45 minutes   Cook Time: 30 - 45 minutes

Ingredients
5 cups quince, peeled, cored, and sliced
1 1/4 cups sour cherries, pitted
2/3 cup granulated sugar
4 tablespoons light brown sugar
2/3 cup cider vinegar
1/2 orange (including rind), sliced thin
2/3 medium onion, small dice
1 teaspoon ground cardamom
1/4 teaspoon ground fenugreek
1/4 cup chopped walnuts

Directions
Combine ingredients, except walnuts, in a medium saucepan. Cook over medium heat, stirring frequently, for 30 - 45 minutes, or until thickened. Take off heat, stir in walnuts, and pour hot into sterilized jars or refrigerator containers.

Chutneys   63

Beth's Farm Kitchen Plum Chutney

Makes 3 - 4 jars (8-ounce)
Prep Time: 35 minutes   Cook Time: 30 - 45 minutes

Ingredients
4 cups plums, pitted and halved
1/4 lemon (including rind), sliced thin
2 apples, cored and small dice
2/3 cup dark raisins
2/3 cup cider vinegar
1/2 cup honey
1/4 teaspoon ground cayenne
1/4 teaspoon ground allspice
1/4 teaspoon ground clove
1/4 teaspoon ground cinnamon
1/4 teaspoon ground cardamom

Directions
Combine ingredients in a medium saucepan. Cook over medium heat, stirring frequently, for 30 - 45 minutes, or until thickened. Take off heat and pour hot into sterilized jars or refrigerator containers.

Slow Food Invades

After a week in Italy on a Slow Food mission, I highly recommend fresh or frozen ravioli filled with pumpkin. Cook according to manufacturer's directions.

Serve with a sauce of butter, sage leaves, and 2 tablespoons **Beth's Farm Kitchen Plum Chutney** that have been sautéed for just a few minutes. Sprinkle with parmesan cheese ... and you are in heaven. Buon appetito!

Hospital Brownies: The Revamp

My first job was at the Greenwich Hospital Coffee Shop. My sister Rita Ann was influential in getting it for me. Even back then, you had to know someone. She has come to my rescue, again, by digging up this recipe.

Preheat oven to 350°F. Mix 2 cups sugar and 4 eggs well. Add 1/2 cup **Beth's Farm Kitchen Plum Chutney** and 1/2 cup sour cream. Mix. Add 4 ounces chocolate melted with 1/4 pound butter and 2 teaspoons vanilla. Add 1 2/3 cups all-purpose flour sifted with 2 teaspoons baking powder and 1/2 teaspoon salt. Add 1 1/2 cups chopped walnuts. Pour into greased 9" x 13" pan. Bake 40 minutes. When knife comes out clean, it's done.

A Chocolate Fancier's Financiers

The big decision with this chutney was whether to give you multiple choices or only one choice of sweets. Our love of chocolate won out, and you are getting chocolate x 2.

Makes 16 pieces
Prep Time: 25 minutes   Cook Time: 12 minutes

Ingredients
2 tablespoons vegetable oil
9 tablespoons butter
1 bar (1 1/8-ounce) bittersweet chocolate
1 cup powdered sugar
1/4 cup, plus 2 tablespoons, all-purpose flour
1/3 cup, plus 1 tablespoon, finely ground almonds
1 egg white
1 teaspoon vanilla
1/2 cup **Beth's Farm Kitchen Plum Chutney**
1/2 teaspoon salt

Directions
Preheat oven to 350º F. Grease financier molds* or mini-cupcake pans with oil. Melt butter over medium-low heat, stirring often, until it turns amber and smells nutty; keep warm. Melt chocolate in a double boiler over low heat and keep warm. In large bowl, sift together sugar and flour. Add almonds and mix with wooden spoon. Add egg white and vanilla, and stir vigorously.

Warm 3 tablespoons butter, pour into batter, and mix well; stir in remaining butter and then stir in chocolate. Fold in chutney. Add salt. Fill molds 3/4 of way with batter. Bake for 12 minutes, rotating pan after 6 minutes. Let cool slightly on baking sheet and then transfer from molds to a cooling rack.

Let cool completely. Serve with tea or frozen yogurt.

* Similar to madeleine molds.

Chutneys   65

Delish Fish Dish

Agrodolce means "sour and sweet" in Italian. You can make an agrodolce sauce with a balsamic vinegar and sugar reduction. Even easier, use our chutney, which already has sugar and vinegar in it. The texture of the fish is enhanced by the flavor of the chutney.

Makes 4 - 6 servings
Prep Time: None   Cook Time: 10 minutes

Ingredients
4 - 6 scrod fillets
2 tablespoons olive oil
2 tablespoons butter
1 cup **Beth's Farm Kitchen Plum Chutney**
1/4 cup white wine

Directions
In a sauté pan, cook fish in oil and butter until tender and flaky. Remove and set aside. Add **Beth's Farm Kitchen Plum Chutney** and wine to sauté pan. Deglaze pan and cook until liquid thickens. Pour over fish and serve.

Words, Words

My first experience with the word "agrodolce" was about three or four years ago, when we started planning the recipes for this book.

Since then, we've been tasting, always tasting. Linda Romeo, the lady in charge of our stoves, said we should do a simple agrodolce with tilapia using **Beth's Farm Kitchen Blazing Tomato Chutney™**.

Simple for her to say! I had to look up the word. But the next Wednesday was "testing day." That winter, Beth's Farm Kitchen invited neighbors in for taste tests. We served tilapia, and it was very well received.

Glamorous Hors d'Oeuvres

Recently, I had an hors d'oeuvre that was a variation on agrodolce, and it opened up another avenue of thought for me.

I love pulled pork but have not done much with it. It is a sweet-and-sour treatment of pork. So from that came pulled pork on a flatbread with a dollop of **Beth's Farm Kitchen Green Tomato Chutney** on top. This led me to think of even more possibilities, such as salmon salad and **Beth's Farm Kitchen Hot Plum Chutney**, and tuna salad with **Beth's Farm Kitchen Cranberry Horseradish Chutney**.

This is a caterer's dream product—something ordinary turned into something extraordinary with ease and ingenuity.

Turkey Agrodolce with a Curry Splash

Turkey was the choice for this agrodolce, but chicken cutlets work as well.

Makes 6 servings
Prep Time: 10 minutes   Cook Time: 50 - 60 minutes

Ingredients
1 small (2 - 3-pound) turkey breast*
6 slices bacon
1 cup **Beth's Farm Kitchen Madras Nectar Chutney**
1/4 cup tomato juice
1/4 cup white wine

Directions
Cover turkey breast with bacon to prevent drying. Roast in preheated 375°F oven for 50 minutes. Test with fork. Juices should run clear, not pink. If pink, bake for another 10 minutes. Remove turkey breast from oven, cover with foil, and let rest.

Add **Beth's Farm Kitchen Madras Nectar Chutney** and remaining ingredients to juices in pan. Scrape bottom of pan to deglaze and continue cooking on stovetop until sauce is reduced by half. Slice turkey breast, pour hot sauce over it, and serve.

Sauce is excellent for leftover turkey anytime.

* You can use turkey cutlets if time is an issue; then just sauté in pan and follow directions on previous page. Turkey breast is less expensive, and bacon adds flavor. There are tradeoffs.

Country Captain Chicken

This dish came into being way back, when the English were navigating the trade waters around the world. The recipe seems to have originated in Bengal or Madras, and its name appears to refer to the captains of the vessels. These men ate well and, when they were in Charleston or Savannah to pick up molasses and drop off slaves, they taught the Southern ladies how to cook their favorite meal. Many myths rolled into one enjoyable story.

Makes 4 servings
Prep Time: 20 minutes   *Cook Time: 45 minutes*

Ingredients
1/2 cup all-purpose flour
Coarse salt and freshly ground black pepper
4 medium chicken breasts with bone out, or cut-up chicken parts
3 tablespoons olive oil
1 medium onion, chopped coarse
1/2 red bell pepper cut into 1/4" strips
1 clove garlic, minced
1 cup **Beth's Farm Kitchen Red Tomato Jam**
1 cup tomato juice
1 cup **Beth's Farm Kitchen Madras Nectar Chutney**
2 teaspoons curry powder
1/2 teaspoon freshly grated ginger
1/4 cup golden raisins or currants
1/4 cup toasted slivered almonds

Directions
Combine flour, salt, and pepper in a bowl. Lightly roll chicken to coat. Prepare fry pan with oil and brown chicken to a light brown, but do not cook fully. Set aside on a platter in 200°F oven. Add onion, bell pepper, and garlic to fry pan with drippings. Sauté until onion is translucent. Add jam, juice, chutney, curry powder, and ginger. Simmer for 15 minutes, covered, until flavors have melded. Add browned chicken and raisins or currants. Simmer for 15 minutes, covered. Remove from heat, place chicken on a platter, pour gravy over chicken, and sprinkle with almonds. Serve with billowy white rice and a salad.

Savory Steak

Grilling is easy and fun. Use this versatile marinade for quick-cooking meat like flank, skirt or hanger steak. Be sure to watch the grill, as the sugar in the chutney could burn. Prepping the grill with no-stick cooking spray before you put the steak on will prevent shredding and sticking.

Ingredients
1/2 cup apple cider or white wine
3 tablespoons mild vegetable oil
1 cup **Beth's Farm Kitchen Zapricot Chutney**
1 - 2 pounds flank, hanger, or skirt steak

Directions
Mix first 3 ingredients in a bowl. Add steak to marinade. Marinate 8 - 12 hours in refrigerator in a plastic storage bag. Heat grill to hot and grill for 4 - 6 minutes per side, depending on thickness of steak. Remove from grill and let rest for 5 minutes. Slice on bias. Serve.

Zany Jellies, Pickles and Then Some

Over the decades, we learned about, read about, or thought about unique and interesting jellies, pickles and relishes. Many did not even exist in stores, yet every product seemed worth introducing. So we took the challenge and introduced several. Happily, most have been successful.

We call this category **Zany Jellies, Pickles and Then Some**.

These are products that have strayed from the beaten path, not true jams, not chutneys. Just in between. "Slightly askew," as Mom would have said.

We use liquid pectin, such as Certo™, for the jellies in this chapter. Liquid pectin produces a clear gel that accentuates the dispersed particles in the product, such as diced habaneros.

Enjoy these original, delicious and versatile Beth's Farm Kitchen Zany Jellies, Pickles and Then Some.

> Mighty Hot Pepper Jelly
> Habanero Jelly
> Garlic Jelly
> Garlic-Rosemary Jelly
> Spicy Corn Relish
> Bread & Butter Pickles
> Red Tomato Jam
> And Then Some

Beth's Farm Kitchen Mighty Hot Pepper Jelly

This jelly has a Southern or Texan flavor. It has a "traditional" pull from both regions. We made **Beth's Farm Kitchen Hot Pepper Jelly** back in the 1980s, but as people's awareness of, and interest in food grew, so did the amount of "heat" they wanted. So, we stepped up to **Beth's Farm Kitchen Mighty Hot Pepper Jelly**. Today, even that doesn't seem so "hot."

We make **Beth's Farm Kitchen Might Hot Pepper Jelly** with red and green bell peppers and jalapeño peppers. Then, we add flavor and "heat" by finishing the job with red pepper flakes. Great taste and not hurtful.

Either of our hot pepper jellies, poured over cream cheese or goat cheese and served with crackers, makes an easy appetizer.

Makes 3 - 4 jars (8-ounce)
Prep Time: 25 minutes   Cook Time: 25 minutes

Ingredients
1/4 cup red bell peppers, small dice
1/4 cup green bell peppers, small dice
5 tablespoons jalapeño peppers, small dice
   (approximately 3 peppers)
1/4 - 1/2 teaspoon red pepper flakes, or to your liking
3/4 cup cider vinegar
2 3/4 cups granulated sugar
1 packet liquid pectin

Directions
Combine peppers, pepper flakes, and vinegar in a medium pot. Bring to a simmer over high heat. Add sugar and stir until it comes back to a boil. Add pectin and bring to last boil. Take off heat, skim, and pour hot into sterilized jars or refrigerator containers.

A Bagel Treat: Sunday Morning Special

Slice fresh bagel. Spread with goat cheese, then white fish salad. Top with **Beth's Farm Kitchen Mighty Hot Pepper Jelly**.

....

Jostling, It's a Jammers Thing

Small bits of fruits, vegetables or herbs—peppers, rosemary, garlic, cherries—are called *floaters* in kitchen lingo. We jammers have come up with many solutions to the problems of the dreaded floaters. We want the bits to be evenly dispersed, so we jostle the jars after they have been filled and set a bit. Basically, this is a shaking motion that helps distribute the ingredients. It is a great upper-arm exercise and can resemble a dance if enough jammers are present. This performance usually takes place at the end of the day.

Hot! Hot! Hot!

Scoville units measure the "hotness" of various foods. The more Scoville units, the hotter the pepper. Here's how the habanero pepper measures up against other peppers:

Pepper	Scoville Units
Jalapeño	2,500 - 8,000
Cayenne	30,000 - 50,000
Habanero	100,000 - 350,000

Beth's Farm Kitchen Habanero Jelly

After a while, even **Beth's Farm Kitchen Mighty Hot Pepper Jelly** wasn't "hot" enough for our customers. So, we decided to make **Beth's Farm Kitchen Habanero Jelly**. The habanero is close to the hottest pepper there is!

Beth's Farm Kitchen Habanero Jelly is so hot that we feel compelled to put a warning on the little serving stick we offer at the tasting table. Despite our efforts, it seems that there is always one young man who wants or needs to show off, and he takes a big dollop of the jelly and is immediately "shocked" at its strength, bringing tears to his eyes and a bruise to his ego.

Makes 3 - 4 jars (8-ounce)
Prep Time: 20 minutes   Cook Time: 25 minutes

Ingredients
1/4 cup yellow bell peppers, small dice
1/4 cup red bell peppers, small dice
1/2 cup habanero peppers, small dice
   (approximately 6 peppers)
3/4 cup cider vinegar
2 3/4 cups granulated sugar
1 packet liquid pectin

Directions
Combine peppers and vinegar in a medium pot. Bring to a simmer over high heat. Add sugar and stir until it comes back to a boil. Add pectin and bring to last boil. Take off heat, skim, and pour hot into sterilized jars or refrigerator containers.

Zany Jellies, Pickles and Then Some

Beth's Farm Kitchen Garlic Jelly

Beth's Farm Kitchen Garlic Jelly has many purposes. One tablespoon in stir-fried vegetables adds the right garlic sweetness to the meal.

This product came directly from **Beth's Farm Kitchen Hot Pepper Jelly**. It uses the same basic recipe, including cider vinegar and sugar. Variations on this jelly can be made easily; try adding horseradish, tarragon or sage.

Makes 3 - 4 jars (8-ounce)
Prep Time: 25 minutes   Cook Time: 25 minutes

Ingredients
1/2 cup garlic, blanched and small dice
3/4 cup cider vinegar
2 3/4 cups granulated sugar
1 packet liquid pectin

Directions
Combine garlic and vinegar in a medium pot. Bring to a simmer over high heat. Add sugar and stir until it comes back to a boil. Add pectin and bring to last boil. Take off heat, skim, and pour hot into sterilized jars or refrigerator containers.

Garlic Bruschetta

Cut crusty Italian bread horizontally or into small slices. Toast lightly in oven. Melt 2 tablespoons **Beth's Farm Kitchen Garlic Jelly** in 1/4 cup olive oil. Brush onto bread, sprinkle with parmesan cheese. Heat in a broiler, oven or toaster oven. Voilà, an elegant, interesting, flavorful appetizer.

Other toppings we like are finely chopped tomatoes, cilantro, basil and diced scallions.

Garlic Jelly Grilling Tips

Brush meats, poultry or fish with a mixture of 1/3 olive oil, 2/3 **Beth's Farm Kitchen Garlic Jelly**, then grill, bake or sauté. So simple, so delicious.

An Interesting Note

We buy our rosemary in season from Stokes Farm in New Jersey. Of course, we need to buy enough to make garlic-rosemary jelly over many months. Back at our kitchens, we strip the rosemary branches, chop the herb in a spice grinder, then freeze quantities for convenient use later.

....

Salad Dressing

Combine 1/3 cup white wine vinegar, 2 tablespoons **Beth's Farm Kitchen Garlic-Rosemary Jelly**, salt and pepper to taste, 1 teaspoon Dijon mustard, 1/3 cup extra virgin olive oil. Shake or whisk briskly and use to dress salad greens. Serve.

Beth's Farm Kitchen Garlic-Rosemary Jelly

The original idea for **Beth's Farm Kitchen Garlic-Rosemary Jelly** came from a 1994 *Gourmet* magazine recipe for Easter Lamb Roast with Garlic Rosemary Jelly. We adapted this recipe to suit our evolving tastes by reducing the amount of garlic and adding white wine vinegar to enhance the mix of flavors.

Since lamb and other meats are popular, **Beth's Farm Kitchen Garlic-Rosemary Jelly** is a consistent best seller.

We take special care to be sure that the rosemary is distributed evenly in each jar, by lightly shaking the jars while the jelly is setting. It's an artisanal technique.

Makes 3 - 4 jars (8-ounce)
Prep Time: 30 minutes   Cook Time: 25 minutes

Ingredients
1/4 cup garlic, blanched and small dice
3/4 cup white wine vinegar
2 3/4 cups granulated sugar
2 tablespoons fresh rosemary, chopped fine
1 packet liquid pectin

Directions
Combine garlic and vinegar in a medium pot. Bring to a simmer over high heat. Add sugar and stir until it comes back to a boil. Add rosemary and pectin and bring to last boil. Take off heat, skim, and pour hot into sterilized jars or refrigerator containers.

Garlic Gingery Pear Chicken

Makes 4 - 6 servings
Prep Time: 5 minutes   *Cook Time: 1 hour and 5 minutes*

Ingredients
1 cup **Beth's Farm Kitchen Gingered Pear Jam**
1/2 cup **Beth's Farm Kitchen Garlic Jelly**
2 tablespoons soy sauce
2 tablespoons rice wine vinegar
1 tablespoon sesame oil
8 - 10 skinless chicken thighs
1 cup chopped scallions

Directions
Preheat oven to 350°F.

Mix all ingredients, except chicken and scallions, together. Toss chicken in mix. Arrange in 9" x 13" baking pan. Sprinkle with scallions. Bake for 1 hour. Adjust oven to broil. Brown chicken under broiler for the final 5 minutes, if desired. Serve hot.

Excellent with fettucine, freekeh or spinach.

Veggie Kabobs

These are easy and scrumptious. The prep work is the hardest part, but put your guests at ease by having them pitch in.

Ingredients
1 each of red, yellow and green peppers, cut to a large dice
10 ounces or 2 per skewer small crimini or regular small
    white mushrooms
2 large red onions, cut into large cubes
Cherry or grape tomatoes, enough for 2 or 3 per skewer
1 cup **Beth's Farm Kitchen Garlic Jelly**
Salt and pepper, to taste

Directions
Soak wooden kabob skewers in water for 45 minutes. Preheat grill. Place veggies in a bowl with jelly. Toss to coat evenly. Build kabobs. Add salt and pepper to taste. Grill until veggies are tender. Serve hot.

Food Culture on the Move

Ancient grains have arrived in NYC. The Greenmarket has been instrumental in getting bakers to use a percentage of local grain in their products. This has brought along with it an awareness of the ancient grains. Each has a unique flavor and excellent nutritional values. My repertoire of *the starch* with dinner has expanded. Sometimes I combine a couple of grains, to create an interesting texture.

Grains are prepared like rice. In general, 2 cups water to 1 cup grain.

Freekeh is a Middle Eastern green wheat, harvested early and roasted. High in vitamins and minerals.

Farro, also called emmer, is mentioned in the Bible. Grown and used widely in Italy, now it is a grain of New York.

Spelt is a close cousin of farro, popular in Europe. We see lots of spelt bread. Try using the grain also.

Buckwheat is a seed, not a true grain. Kasha is toasted buckwheat groats; it is a non-gluten product.

Quinoa, a staple of Peru, Bolivia and Chile, is gluten-free, high in protein, and easy to cook. It's available red or black. The black looks good on a plate with flounder and a green veggie.

Wild rice is a seed but used as a grain. It takes longer to cook than other grains.

Try any or all of these grains instead of rice or potatoes with your dinner. Each one has a distinctive, robust flavor you'll enjoy.

Garlic-Rosemary BBQ Spare Ribs

Makes 4 - 6 servings
Prep Time: 10 minutes   Cook Time: 3 - 4 hours

Ingredients
1 rack of pork spare ribs (approximately 5 pounds)
Salt and pepper, to taste
1 cup **Beth's Farm Kitchen Garlic-Rosemary Jelly**
1/2 - 1 bottle (12-ounce) beer or pale ale; we like pale ale for
   added flavor

Directions
Preheat oven to 250ºF.

Place pork ribs on 1 piece of aluminum foil in 11" x 13" baking sheet with 1" - 1 1/2" sides.

Season with salt and pepper.

Mix 1/2 cup **Beth's Farm Kitchen Garlic-Rosemary Jelly** with beer or ale and spread liberally on pork.

With a second piece of aluminum foil make a crimped package with pork inside.

Place in oven to cook for 3 - 4 hours, or until meat is tender and slips easily from bones.

Remove meat from oven and set oven on broil.

Remove top layer of aluminum foil and brush all parts of ribs with remaining **Beth's Farm Kitchen Garlic-Rosemary Jelly**. Be generous. The more jelly, the better the flavor!

When broiler is ready, broil ribs until they become shiny and golden. Serve hot.

Note: You can also slow cook your ribs on a grill. It gives a great smoky, grilled flavor. If you grill, keep heat moderate for the first 3 - 4 hours and slightly increase heat for last 15 minutes of finishing ribs. Crock pot is another way to go.

Zany Jellies, Pickles and Then Some   75

A Unique Corn Relish, Hits All the Right Notes

Beth's Farm Kitchen Spicy Corn Relish is unique. It is less sweet than the classic Pennsylvania Dutch type and also different from the sweeter, thicker Midwestern genre. **Beth's Farm Kitchen Spicy Corn Relish** proudly kicks up its heels—a little sweet, a little hot, a little smoky. It hits all the right notes.

Beth's Farm Kitchen Spicy Corn Relish

Makes 3 - 4 jars (8-ounce)
Prep Time: 25 minutes   Cook Time: 10 minutes

Ingredients
3 cups corn, off the cob
1 medium onion, small dice
1/4 cup red bell pepper, small dice
1/4 cup green bell pepper, small dice
1/4 cup celery, small dice
1 whole cherry pepper, chopped
1 cup white vinegar
1/4 cup granulated sugar
2 tablespoons fresh cilantro, chopped
1/2 teaspoon mustard powder
1/2 teaspoon celery seed
1/2 teaspoon mustard seed
1/4 teaspoon red pepper flakes
1/4 teaspoon fresh horseradish, chopped
1/4 teaspoon ground chipotle
1/8 teaspoon turmeric

Directions
Combine all ingredients in a large saucepan. Bring to a simmer over medium heat. Take off heat and pour hot into sterilized jars or refrigerator containers. Use a wooden skewer or chopstick to take any air bubbles out of jars. Cover contents with brine.

Spicy Corn Relish, Always a Good Idea

- Toss 2 tablespoons into quick green salad for added crunch.

- Hot dog topped with spicy corn relish, a home run!

- Add texture to tuna salad with spicy corn relish.

- A breakfast taco: scrambled eggs, queso blanco, and spicy corn relish.

- Mac 'n' cheese with spicy corn relish, that's the ticket!

- Make tomatillo salsa with spicy corn relish. Wow!

- Give burgers a new flavor zing. Top with a mixture of **Beth's Farm Kitchen Blazing Tomato Chutney** and **Beth's Farm Kitchen Spicy Corn Relish**.

Varieties of Vinegars

White distilled: Distilled from ethyl alcohol. Used in pickle-making.

Cider: America's favorite, tangy and fruity.

Rice: Mild, used primarily in Asian-style foods.

Red and white wine: Tangy, used in marinades and vinaigrettes.

Balsamic: Dark, complex, slightly sweet. Originated in Modena, Italy.

Malt: Preferred by the English, has a lemony flavor.

From here, you go to **flavored vinegars** and there is no limit.

Cooking Lessons from Friends

Early on in life, I did lots of cooking with friends: Ski houses, beach houses and my parents' house. One benefit of all this cooking and eating with friends is the memories. This corn bread is an excellent example; it reminds me of Marcy, who made it for our ski pals. The corn bread I knew was served with lots of butter, and definitely did not have hot peppers. What was she doing to corn bread? She added some heat and a great deal of flavor. Marcy turned me around, and we will do it to you, too. Eat up, enjoy, and make some memories of your own!

Spicy, Cheesy Corn Bread

Makes 8 servings
Prep Time: 15 minutes   Cook Time: 20 minutes

Ingredients
1 box (8-ounce) corn-muffin mix
1 cup **Beth's Farm Kitchen Spicy Corn Relish** (drained)
1/3 cup plain yogurt
1 egg, beaten
1 cup shredded cheddar cheese
1/2 cup **Beth's Farm Kitchen Mighty Hot Pepper Jelly**

Directions
Preheat oven to 400°F. Spray a square, 8" x 8" pan with cooking oil.

In a large bowl, combine corn-muffin mix and relish. Add yogurt, egg and cheese; stir. Do not overmix. Pour into pan. Bake 20 minutes or until center is firm and top is golden.

Remove from oven, prick all over top with a testing stick or toothpick, then brush with **Beth's Farm Kitchen Mighty Hot Pepper Jelly**. Serve warm.

Note: This bread is great with Beth's Farm Kitchen Cowboy Chili!

Beth's Farm Kitchen Bread & Butter Pickles

The best bread and butter pickles have just the right combination of fresh, small cucumbers, onions, vinegar, mustard seed and turmeric. I've worked for years to perfect this recipe, and I always stress the importance of the freshness and size of the cukes. It is very hard to crisp up old or badly stored cucumbers, so instead of pickling them, use them in a relish. Remember, quality ingredients always show!

Makes 3 - 4 jars (8-ounce)
Prep Time: 30 minutes, plus 3 hours on ice
Cook Time: 15 minutes

Ingredients
2 pounds Kirby cucumbers, sliced thin into rounds (skin on)
1/2 onion, sliced thin
4 teaspoons Kosher or pickling salt (not iodized!)
Ice (about one tray's worth)
1 1/3 cups granulated sugar
1/2 teaspoon turmeric
1/3 teaspoon celery seed
2 teaspoons mustard seed
1 1/2 cups cider vinegar

Directions
Mix cucumbers, onion and salt with ice and let sit for 3 hours. Drain cucumbers and onion in a colander and rinse with cold water. In a large pot, combine all other ingredients and bring to a boil. Add cucumbers and onion, bring just to a boil, and remove from heat. Ladle vegetables into sterilized jars or refrigerator containers, then pour hot brine over them to cover. Use a wooden skewer or chopstick to take any air bubbles out of jars.

Bread & Butter Pickles

Delicious so many ways ...

- Chop pickles into yolk mixture with mustard for the best deviled eggs ever.

- Add to tuna sandwich for crunch.

- Eat straight from the jar.

- Add to potato salad.

- Chop fine, add to mayo or yogurt for a tried fish dip.

Spice Notes

A history of the unusual spices in this chapter ...

Chipotle: These peppers are smoked jalapeño chili peppers. The Aztecs smoked them because the walls of these peppers are thick and this was the best way to store them.

Turmeric: A spice with a peppery, bitter flavor that smells like orange and ginger. Used in ballpark mustard and in curries and pickles. A unique feature, also used to dye fabric!

Cayenne pepper: A hot, pungent powder from chilies that originated in a town of the same name in French Guiana.

Cuban Sandwich

Makes 4 - 6 servings
Prep Time: 5 minutes   Cook Time: 8 - 10 minutes

Ingredients
6 panini, ciabatta or long, flat, crusty loaf of bread
1 cup horseradish mustard
1 cup **Beth's Farm Kitchen Bellow Yellow Chutney**
3/4 pound sliced pork
3/4 pound sliced ham
3/4 pound sliced Swiss cheese
1 cup **Beth's Farm Kitchen Bread & Butter Pickles**
1 cup olive oil

Directions
Preheat a cast-iron skillet or griddle over medium-high heat.

Slice bread. On one side, spread mustard; on other side, spread **Beth's Farm Kitchen Bellow Yellow Chutney**. Layer meats, cheese and pickles onto sandwiches.

Brush skillet with olive oil, brown sandwiches on both sides, weighting each side of sandwich on top with a plate or smaller pan. Brown until cheese is melted. Serve hot. Napkins needed!

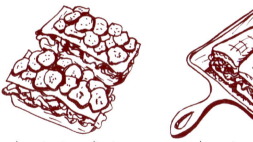

layering ingredients   *browning sandwich*

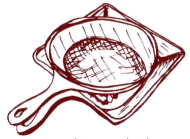

weighting sandwich

Zany Jellies, Pickles and Then Some   79

Pickled Vegetables

Beth's Farm Kitchen Adapt-a-Recipe for Dilly Beans, Dilly Carrots and Veggies

Use this clever, basic recipe to make many different wholesome treats.

Makes 3 - 4 jars (8-ounce)

Ingredients
For Each Pound of Vegetables
1/4 teaspoon cayenne pepper, or to taste
1 clove garlic
1 sprig dill

For Brine
2 cups water
2 1/2 cups white vinegar
1/4 cup Kosher salt

Directions
Combine ingredients for brine and bring to boil over high heat in a medium pot. Put cayenne, garlic and dill in sterilized jars or refrigerator containers. Pack the vegetables into the jars and trim the ends so the correct head space is allowed. Cover with hot brine.

Beans and carrots: Use dill, cayenne and garlic.

Asparagus: Only put dill in brine with veggie (no cayenne or garlic).

Fiddlehead ferns: Only put garlic with veggie (no cayenne or dill).

Ramps: Don't put anything with veggie.

Turnips and radishes: Only put cayenne and dill with veggie (no garlic).

Garlic scapes: Only put dill with veggie (no cayenne or garlic).

Pickled cherry peppers: Don't put anything with veggie.

Dilly Beans

Dilly beans are spicy, pickled green beans with garlic and dill, another traditional, Americana item. They seem to be a natural product of the "canning generation," a way to enjoy nutritious vegetables regardless of season. An excellent, tasty concept.

Beth's Farm Kitchen used regular green beans for several years, but because they naturally grow crooked and have irregular shapes, they were a challenge to our patience. Then we found Alvinah Frey and Rick Bishop and their "haricots verts," an excellent and efficient bean choice. The next improvement was when science and Samascott's Orchard perfected growing straight-arrow green beans. Now the only trick is to buy and can enough in season. Buying local takes planning.

Dilly Carrots

Dilly carrots appear in most old cookbooks, so we decided to try our luck. The trick, apparently, seems to be "crispness" after canning. Dill and cayenne pepper are the ingredients that make the difference. We use the big, "horse" carrots because 8-ounce jars require a lot of trimming by hand. While there is waste, the large carrots keep it to a minimum.

....

An Excellent Leftover Idea

Use the trimmed carrot tips to make the Carrot Nectar Soup on Page 45. It's one of our favorites and will be yours, too!

The Perfect Sushi Pretender

Easy, ideal for picnics, buffets or on-the-go lunches, because this "sushi" needs no refrigeration. Simply delicious.

Makes: 6 - 8 rolls
Prep Time: 10 minutes   *Cook Time: 30 minutes*

Ingredients
1 package nori wrap
White or brown rice, cooked and cooled
1 cup **Beth's Farm Kitchen Cranberry Horseradish Chutney**
1 cup **Beth's Farm Kitchen Dilly Carrots**
1 cup **Beth's Farm Kitchen Dilly Beans**

Directions
Place a bamboo mat on table. Put a sheet of plastic wrap over bamboo mat, then nori with shiny side face down, on mat. With damp hands, grab cooked rice and spread onto nori. The layer of rice should be thin enough so that you can see nori underneath. Leave about 1/2" of space at edge of nori farther from you. Rub a bit of warm water on it. This will help sides of nori stick together.

Spread with a generous layer of **Beth's Farm Kitchen Cranberry Horseradish Chutney**. Line up a row (2 each) of **Beth's Farm Kitchen Dilly Carrots** and **Beth's Farm Kitchen Dilly Beans** on nori/rice/chutney closer to you. Roll away from you, using mat and plastic wrap as a guide for nori. Roll onto plastic wrap to create a tube and seal the ends. To serve, unwrap and cut into individual pieces.

A pretty little package of savory food.

Beth's Farm Kitchen Red Tomato Jam

This is a classic European breakfast jam. Our recipe is equally delicious as a spread or an ingredient.

Makes 4 - 5 jars (8-ounce)
Prep Time: 25 minutes   Cook Time: 20 minutes

Ingredients
3 large tomatoes, medium dice (approximately 1 1/2 pounds)
1/4 lemon, sliced thin
1/4 teaspoon cinnamon
1 cup granulated sugar
2 teaspoons Pomona's Universal Pectin
   (plus 2 teaspoons calcium water)

Directions
In a medium pot, bring calcium water, tomatoes, lemon and cinnamon to a boil. In a separate bowl, combine sugar and pectin. Mix vigorously. Slowly add pectin mixture to boiling pot of tomato mixture while stirring vigorously. Return to rolling boil, check set and let cool. Pour into sterilized jars or refrigerator containers.

Reminder: Tomatoes are fruits, just as rhubarb is a vegetable.

Romeo's Curried Chicken

Makes 4 - 6 servings
Prep Time: 30 minutes
Cook Time: 25 minutes

In a sauté pan over a medium heat, combine 2 tablespoons butter, 1 thin-sliced onion, 2 cups carrots, small dice, 2 cups chopped cauliflower and 3 minced garlic cloves until lightly browned.

Add 2 tablespoons curry powder, sauté 1 - 2 minutes.

Add 1 cup chicken stock, 1 cup unsweetened coconut milk and 1 cup **Beth's Farm Kitchen Red Tomato Jam**. Reduce liquid over high heat until almost evaporated. Set aside.

In another sauté pan, cook 2 whole chicken boneless breasts cut into 1" cubes with 2 tablespoons butter for 5 minutes. Season with salt and pepper. Add chicken to vegetable mix, stir, and serve hot over freekeh.

More Jamming Tips from Beth's Farm Kitchen

Pots and Pans and Other Paraphernalia

Be extremely aware of the weight of your pots when making jams and chutneys. Bottoms should be thick—both to withstand the continuous high heat we use when cooking jams and chutneys, and to maintain the pots' own integrity. I have used Farberware pots (12- and 16-quart) for 30 years. Copper pots are ideal for jam, because the metal conducts heat very well, right up the sides of the pots. They are quite expensive, but, if you use only one, you will enjoy it.

Heat-resistant handles are a great convenience, but really efficient hot pads are EXTREMELY important. Do not use wet hot pads for anything.

We have always used wooden spoons. You should also. Wood does not conduct heat. A metal spoon in a jam pot on the burner will get so hot that it will burn anyone who touches it. I see wooden spoons as a symbol of how committed I am to making artisanal jam. Do not use plastic spoons or scrapers, as they usually melt.

Another piece of equipment that I like, particularly for the no-sugar spreads and the jams without added pectin, is the fat-splatter screen. We have a low ceiling in our kitchen, and it is often splatted with apple butter, so we wash it once a week with a mop. The floor gets washed everyday.

Use canning jars to jar jams and chutneys. They are made of tempered glass, which can freeze or boil. Mayonnaise jars cannot take the heat. Never use a canning lid more than once. The plastisol ring on the inside of the lid is designed for one use only.

Plastic containers must be reusable food-storage containers. Glass storage containers are not good for canning. They are not made of tempered glass, as canning jars are.

Always sanitize your equipment, including jars, other containers, and kitchen surfaces, before getting started. We recommend using a solution of 1 tablespoon of bleach for every 1 gallon of water. Lay out everything you are going to need before you start, as they do in cooking shows. This is your *mise en place* or, as my friend Ruby says, your "mess in one place." Your *mise en place* should include a ladle, a funnel, paper towels, small plates for checking sets, a regular teaspoon, jar lifters, lid lifters, tongs, hot pads, wooden spoons, and aprons. When making jam, you cannot get distracted, because boil-overs and charred pots are difficult and time-consuming to rectify. They do happen, and have happened, to all jam-makers. Avoid this pitfall!

You will need a variety of pots and pans. Here are the ones I use, along with their sizes.

Small pots hold 1 quart.

Medium pots hold 2 quarts.

Large pots hold 3 quarts (ideal for making jam or chutney).

Extra-large pots hold 6 quarts (1 1/2 gallons).

Sauté pans have high sides and a long handle.

Skillets (or fry pans) come in 6", 8", 10", and 12" diameters.

Cookie sheets have one turned-up side: 12"x 14".

Sheet pans (or baking pans) have 1" sides: 11"x 14" x 1", 11" x 16"x 1".

Cake pans are round, and are 8 or 9 in diameter.

Baking pans can be square (8" x 8" or 9" x 9") or oval (11" x 5").

Canning pots: You can use any pasta pot with a wire cake rack in the bottom, to keep the jars from touching the bottom. You need a lid and, when the pot is boiling and the jars are in it, there must be 1" of water above them.

Fruits and Vegetables

Clean all fruit when it comes into your house. Try to buy fruit at a farm or a farmers' market. The vast majority of apples at farmers' markets are not waxed. This is a good thing. Apples are waxed so they can travel long distances.

Make the recipes as we recommend. Just because you have a little more fruit, do not change the recipe to make it fit. Freeze the extra for later use on oatmeal, on ice cream, or in a smoothie.

The fruits that generally need peeling before freezing are pears, peaches, and tomatoes. Freeze peaches in the amounts you will use for one batch of jam.

To freeze rhubarb, as we do, wash it well, trim its roots and leaves, and chop it into 1/2" dice. Freeze in plastic freezer bags in batches or multiples of batches.

We have had to pit cherries many times, and there is no easy, fast way to do it at home. We have sour cherries pitted at a commercial plant and a warning on all our cherry-containing products, "Pits Possible."

In Conclusion

Are you getting the idea that this is a labor-intensive profession? You will love homemade jam even more if you recognize this truth.

There are many more fruits to be discussed, but we are counting on you to look up the information or call us. The book that we rely on for the details of canning is *The Ball Blue Book*. Buy it and follow it. If you have questions, we will be happy to help. I want you to enjoy the food in your life.

Local Farms Supplying Beth's Farm Kitchen with Fruits and Vegetables

Berried Treasures Farms
Blue Star Farms
Cahoon Farms
Cherry Lane Farm of Roadtown
Cherry Ridge Orchards
Deep Mountain Maple
Ekerton Hill Farm
Emmerich Greenhouses
Fishkill Farms
G.M. Allen and Sons
Gonzalez Farm
Hector Perez
Hoeffner Farms
Heron's Roost Farm
Katchkie Farm
Kernan Farms
Locust Grove
Maxwell Farms
Montgomery Place Orchard
Mountain Sweet Berries
Norwich Meadows
Paffenroth Gardens
Phillips Orchards
Red Jacket Orchard
Samascott Orchards
Stokes Farm
S & S.O. Produce Farms
The Berry Farm
The Cheerful Cherry Farm
Wilklow Orchards
Wild Hive Bakery
Windfall Farms

Local Farm Producers of Great Food Used in Beth's Farm Kitchen Recipes

Blue Moon Fish
Body and Soul/CounterNYC
Bread Alone Bakery
Cato Corner Farm
Cayuga Pure Organic
DiPaola Turkeys
Flying Pigs Farm
Grazin' Angus
Great Performances
Hudson Valley Duck
Hudson Valley Homestead
Milk Thistle Dairy
Not Just Rugelach
Our Daily Bread
Pura Vida Fisheries
Quattro's Game Farm
Rockhill Bakery
Ronnybrook Dairy
Silvermine Apiary
Tremblay Apiaries
Twin Spruce Apiary
Valley Shepherd Creamery
Violet Hill Farm

Beth's Farm Kitchen Products

WHERE TO BUY THEM

Columbia County

Blackwood & Brower
The Berry Farm
Chatham Real Food Coop
Community Food Compact
Cascades Café
The Farmer's Wife
Goold Orchards
Hawthorne Valley Farm Store
Hudson-Chatham Winery
Otto's Market
Our Daily Bread
The Rosery Flower Shop
Samascott's Greenhouses
Stone Wall Hill Farm
Taconic Orchards

Hudson Valley

Gift Works
Gigi's Market
Hudson Milk Company
Homespun Foods
L'Anjou French Pastry
McEnroe's Organic Farm
Migiliorelli's Farm
Peach Grove Inn
Quattro's Market
Red Devon Restaurant
Rusty Tractor Farmer's Market
Table Local Market
Wild Hive Bakery

WHERE TO EAT THEM

Columbia County

Inn at Green River
Le Gamin Country
Local 111

Connecticut

Kent Goods
Paley's Market

Massachusetts

Guido's

Maine

The Cheese Iron

New Jersey

Alan's Orchard
Ester's Treats
Not Just Rugelach

New York State

Honest Weight Food Coop
Lewis Waite Farm
Rockhill Bakehouse
The Pampered Cow
Basis Farm to Chef

Manhattan

BUY:

BLT @ the Ritz Carlton
Dean and Deluca
Silvermoon Bakery

EAT:

Broslin Bar & Ace Hotel
Café Henri
The City Bakery
Ground Support
Henry's Restaurant
Le Grainne Café
Sheraton Hotel @ 52nd Street
The Spotted Pig
Two Little Red Hens
Wilfie and Nell
Zoë Café

Brooklyn

BUY:

Cobblestone Foods
General Greene Grocery
Marlow and Daughters
Union Market
Bedford Cheese Shop

EAT:

Egg
Le Gamin: Vanderbilt, Franklin

You can also find our products at the following New York City Greenmarket locations:

- Union Square (Wednesdays, Fridays and Saturdays)
- Columbia University – 114th Street and Broadway (Thursdays and Sundays)
- 97th Street and Columbus Avenue (Fridays)

… and online, at www.bethsfarmkitchen.com.

Glossary

Agrodolce: Sweet and sour. A term created from the Italian words "agro" (meaning "sour") and "dolce" (meaning "sweet"). "Agridulce" in Spanish.

Artisan: A person skilled in a manual art.

Artisanal: An adjective that identifies hand-crafted food products, such as cheese or Beth's Farm Kitchen products.

Batter: A combination of dry ingredients (such as flour, sugar and seasonings) and one or more liquids (such as oil, milk, water and juice). Example, pancake batter.

Blanching: An easy and traditional cooking method typically used to prepare foods for freezing. Fruits or vegetables are plunged into boiling water for a short time, then into ice-cold water to stop the cooking process. Blanching firms and protects the texture of foods, enriches their color and flavor, and loosens skins for easy peeling.

Braise: To cook meat slowly in a covered pot or pan containing a small amount of liquid. Often, to enrich its flavor, the meat is browned by cooking briefly on high heat before braising.

Calcium water: A mixture that helps jam to gel. It is made by mixing the calcium powder included in a package of Pomona's Universal Pectin with water. Follow the manufacturer's directions precisely. *(See "Pectin.")*

Caramelize: To heat sugar beyond the melting point until it becomes brown and has a caramel flavor.

Chutney: A blend of fruit, vinegar, sugar and spices. The word comes from the East Indian word "chatni." Chutney flavors range from very mild to very hot, depending on the ingredients. Texture can range from smooth to chunky, also depending on the ingredients. Chutney is an ideal accompaniment to many foods and an excellent ingredient.

Conserve: A jam made with two or more fruits, plus either raisins or nuts, or both. Excellent on toast or biscuits.

Cream: The fat contained in milk. Half & Half is made up of milk (50%) and cream (50%) and contains 10 - 12% fat, light cream contains 18 - 30% fat, light whipping cream has 30 - 36% fat, and heavy whipping cream has 36-40% fat.

Cream: To combine ingredients, such as butter and sugar, until the mixture is as smooth as cream.

Curry paste: It comes in red, yellow and green and is used in Thai food. You can make a batch yourself, but you can buy Petak's brand at many local ethnic food markets.

Cut in: To distribute fat, such as butter, in dry ingredients by using two knives, a pastry blender, or a blending fork. In this method, the fat is literally "cut in," so that small bits of fat are covered or coated with the dry ingredients. This makes the dough more tender, which is where the word "shortening" comes from, and helps produce a crisp pastry or other product.

Dal: A high-protein mix of pulses (bean families) served in India and Pakistan. As we look for more nutritious foods, we will be eating more beans and lentils, as they have for thousands of years on the Indian peninsula. Other spellings: daal, dhal, dahl, dhaal.

Dash: A small amount (less than 1/4 teaspoon). A sprinkle.

Deglaze: To heat a small amount of stock, wine or water in a pan to dissolve and collect the browned, flavorful bits of food that remain after food has been sautéed. The deglazed liquid is an excellent ingredient for gravy or other sauces.

Dice: To cut or chop into same-size pieces. Small dice, 1/4" pieces; medium dice 1/2" pieces; large dice, 3/4 - 1" pieces.

Dough: A thick mixture of flour, liquid, fat, eggs, leavening and other ingredients that is worked by pushing or pulling by hand or machine.

Egg wash: A mixture of whole egg, yolk, or white and a small amount of water or milk. The wash is brushed over breads, pastry, and other baked goods before baking; it helps to produce a shiny color on them.

Fry: To cook over direct heat, with fat, to add flavor. There are two basic frying methods—pan-frying and deep-frying. In pan-frying, the quantity of fat in the pan comes half-way up the product you are frying; in deep-frying, the quantity of fat in the pan covers the product completely.

Garam masala: An Indian spice mixture that varies by region. You can make it yourself or buy it through Amazon.com. We can buy it at local Indian markets in New York City.

Glaze: To cover with a transparent coating of jelly, syrup, thickened juice, or caramel.

Jam: A cooked mixture of fruit, sugar, and sometimes pectin that is smooth or has soft chunks of fruit. Used as a spread or filling for cookies, pastries, or other desserts.

Jar: A glass container. Most Beth's Farm Kitchen products are available in 8-ounce jars; a few come in 16-ounce jars.

Jelly: A firm, clear, cooked mixture of fruit juice, sugar, and sometimes pectin. Used as a glaze, spread, or filling for doughnuts, cookies or cakes.

Julienne: To cut food into thin, matchstick-size strips, about 1/8" thick. Julienned oranges are used to make **Beth's Farm Kitchen Orange Marmalade**, for example.

Knead: To mix ingredients by pressing, then folding and stretching, and then pressing again.

Marinade: A liquid used to cover food to add flavor to it and/or tenderize it.

Marinate: To use a marinade to add flavor to food and/or tenderize it.

Marmalade: A preserve made with citrus fruit, including the rind and pulp, plus sugar. **Beth's Farm Kitchen Triple Fruit Marmalade** is made from a blend of grapefruit, orange, and lemon.

Mince: To cut food into very small pieces, of about 1/8".

Organic: A term used to describe food grown and processed using only natural materials and without the use of any manufactured chemicals, artificial coloring or chemical flavoring, or other additives.

Pan-broil: To cook meats or fish quickly using high, direct heat. The food is put into a heavy, ungreased, or lightly greased frying pan and drippings are removed if they form during cooking.

Parboil: To cook dense food partially by boiling it in water for a short time. Parboiled ingredients, such as carrots, can then be combined with ingredients that require less cooking, such as bean sprouts, for stir-frying or other quick-cook recipes. Very similar to blanching.

Pare: To remove the outer skin or surface of a fruit or vegetable.

Pectin: A natural gelatin or thickening ingredient in fruits and vegetables. When pectin is combined with sugar, acid and heat, it creates jams, jellies and preserves. Sometimes additional pectin is needed to create the correct texture for the finished product. There are two forms of pectin used for cooking: Liquid pectin is usually made from apples, dry pectin from citrus fruits or apples. Pomona's Universal Pectin is our powdered pectin of choice. It is sold by Workstead Industries, P.O. Box 1083, Greenfield, Massachusetts 01302. You can also contact the company by e-mail (at info@pomonapectin.com), or by calling its JAMLINE (413-772-6816) and speaking with Connie Sumberg.

Pinch: A tiny amount. Literally, the amount of an ingredient, such as salt, that can be picked up by pinching the thumb and forefinger together.

Poach: To cook food gently in stock, lightly salted water, or a sugar syrup just below the boiling point. Poaching helps develop the unique flavors of foods, and can enrich those flavors by incorporating the mild taste of the poaching liquid.

Preheat: To heat the oven to the correct temperature for cooking before putting the food in it.

Preserve: A jam made preserving the shape of the fruit.

Sambal oelek: A blend of chilies that is used to add flavor and "heat" to recipes.

Sauté: To cook with just enough fat to keep the food from sticking to the pan.

Score: To make shallow, diagonal cuts on the surface of meats or breads. Scoring is used to decorate, to help marinating meats absorb flavor, and to allow excess fat to drain during cooking.

Sear: To seal in the meat juices by cooking the meat quickly over very high heat.

Set: To "test for set" means to look at a spoonful of jam that has been dropped on a cool plate. If the jam spreads out, it is not set; if the jam forms a mound and you can move the plate without moving the jam, the jam is set. We often put the plate with jam on it in the freezer for a few moments, because our kitchen can get so hot that the set will never show otherwise.

Sift: To pass dry ingredients, such as flour or confectioner's sugar, through a sieve to remove lumps and preserve the ingredients' natural consistency. It prevents "packing" or inaccurate measuring.

Simmer: To cook in 185°F water, with bubbles breaking just below the surface.

Steam: To cook by placing food over boiling water in a covered pan. Steaming helps preserve the natural flavor, nutritional value, shape, and texture of food.

Sterilize: To clean an open jar with a bleach solution (to prepare the jar for filling), or to clean a closed jar by placing it through a hot-water bath. To remove bacteria.

Stir-fry: To cook quickly in a hot pan that has a small amount of fat. Ingredients are prepared by being cut into even-sized pieces and then, if necessary, parboiled. When the pan is hot, the ingredients are put into it, then stirred constantly so they cook evenly.

Whip: To increase volume by beating or stirring briskly to incorporate air.

Glossary 93

Recipe Index

JAMS	Category	Use(s)	Page No.
Beth's Farm Kitchen Basic Jam with Added Pectin	Jam		12
Beth's Farm Kitchen Basic Jam without Added Pectin	Jam		13
Jam Tarts	Dessert	Snack, cookie	14
PB&J Over Time	Sandwich	Lunch, snack	14
Chocolate Frosting	Cake frosting	Brownie frosting, cake filling, quick fudge	15
Delectably Dark Chocolate Cake	Dessert		15
Nancy's Rhubarb Coffee Cake	Dessert	Coffee cake	16
Jammy Baked Apples	Dessert	Snack	17
Orange on Orange Sweet Loaf	Cake	Vegan, breakfast, coffee cake	17
Aunt Gilda's Plum Crumb Cake	Dessert	Coffee cake	18
Duck Breasts with Chutney and Jam	Poultry	Main course	19
Lemon Blueberry Pie	Dessert		19
Ginger Peachy Clafoutis	Dessert	Brunch	20
Christian's Sautéed Shrimp	Dinner	Seafood	20
Peach Jam Cobbler	Dessert	Breakfast	21
Beth's Farm Kitchen Basic No-Sugar Spread	Spread	No-sugar jam	22
Pork Glaze with Beth's Farm Kitchen Apple Butter	Meat sauce	No-sugar apple butter	23
Beth's Farm Kitchen Basic Chunky Applesauce	Fruit	No-sugar jam	23
Beth's Farm Kitchen Orange Marmalade	Marmalade	Basic recipe, jam	24
Crêpes Suzette à la Beth's Farm Kitchen	Dessert	Snack	25

JAMS (continued)	Category	Use(s)	Page No.
Saucy Pork Cutlets	Dinner	Pork, Meyer Lemon Marmalade, Chili Cranberry Chutney	26
Tangy Marinade for Chicken or Lamb Chops	Marinade	Lamb/chicken sauce, Bitter Orange Marmalade	26

CHUTNEYS	Category	Use(s)	Page No.
Beth's Farm Kitchen Blazing Tomato Chutney™	Chutney		29
Cowboy Chili	Main dish	Blazing Tomato Chutney™	30
Fish Story Retold	Main dish	Bluefish, seafood	30
Chez Brennan Meatloaf	Dinner	Blazing Tomato Chutney™, snack, lunch	31
Spaghetti Puttanesca	Main dish	Pasta	32
Pasta e Fagioli Soup	Soup	Main dish, pasta	33
Savory Gruyère Clafoutis	Main dish	Appetizer, lunch	34
Breezy Brisket	Main dish	Beef	34
Beth's Farm Kitchen Golden Pear Chutney	Chutney		35
Chutney Upside-Down Cake	Dessert	Brunch	36
No Oven Tonight	Chicken	Main course	37
Golden Braised Lamb	Main dish	Lamb	37
Beth's Farm Kitchen Hot Plum Chutney	Chutney		38
Elegantly Dressed Pork Tenderloin	Meal	Pork, main course	39
Beth's Farm Kitchen Cranberry-Lime Chutney	Chutney		40
Summer Salad	Salad		40
Salmon with a Cranberry Slant	Seafood	Main course, salmon	41
Beth's Farm Kitchen Chili Cranberry Chutney	Chutney		41
Beth's Farm Kitchen Cranberry Horseradish Chutney	Chutney		42
Classic Monte Cristo Sandwich with Horseradish Twist	Main dish	Brunch	43
Beth's Farm Kitchen Madras Nectar Chutney	Chutney		44
Carrot Nectar Soup	Soup	Lunch, carrots	45

CHUTNEYS (continued)	Category	Use(s)	Page No.
Beth's Farm Kitchen Peach Chutney	Chutney		46
Tamale Treats	Snack	Lunch	47
Grilled Cheese and Chutney Sandwich	Lunch	Brunch	47
New-Style Roasted Vegetables with Cilantro Yogurt Sauce	Vegetables	Side dish, lunch	48
Saucy 'n' Savory	Main dish	Sausage	49
Beth's Farm Kitchen Hot 'n' Spicy Chutney	Chutney		49
Beth's Farm Kitchen Delta Road Chutney	Chutney		50
Life is Easier with Chutney	Salad	Appetizer, lunch, chicken salad	50
Grilled Peach and Chutney Salad	Salad	Vegetarian, vegan	51
Sweet, Sweet Potato Salad	Salad	Vegetarian, vegan	52
Beth's Farm Kitchen Green Tomato Chutney	Chutney		53
Vegetable Turnover: The Best New Snack Food	Snack	Vegetarian, vegan	54
Your Own Dough	Turnover dough		54
Sauce Notes	Sauces		55
Chicken Tenders: Sauced and Served	Main dish	Appetizer	55
Beth's Farm Kitchen Ragin' Rhubarb Chutney	Chutney		56
Beth's Farm Kitchen Rhubarb Chutney	Chutney		56
Sauces and Chutney	Sauce		56
Veggie Salad à la Beth's	Salad	Vegetarian, vegan	57
Ragin' Cajun Shrimp Po' Boy	Main dish	Lunch, seafood, shrimp	57
Goat Cheese and Greens Pizza	Dinner	Snack, brunch	58
Dazzling Dip	Dip		58
How to Make a Samosa	Lunch	Snack, brunch	59
Don's Dal	Snack	Lunch, brunch	59
Beth's Farm Kitchen Bellow Yellow Chutney	Chutney		60
Mint-Cilantro Chutney from Monica Bhide	Chutney		61
Broccoli Rabe and Chutney Dance the Couscous Together	Main dish	Side dish	61
Beth's Farm Kitchen Zapricot Chutney	Chutney		62
Potato and Sausage Salad	Salad	Sausage, potatoes	62
Dining with Doris	Appetizer		63

CHUTNEYS (continued)	Category	Use(s)	Page No.
Beth's Farm Kitchen Quincherry Chutney	Chutney		63
Beth's Farm Kitchen Plum Chutney	Chutney		64
Slow Food Invades	Main course	Pasta, ravioli	64
Hospital Brownies: The Revamp	Dessert	Snack	65
A Chocolate Fancier's Financiers	Dessert	Snack	65
Delish Fish Dish	Seafood	Main course	66
Words, Words	Seafood	Blazing Tomato Chutney™ with tilapia	66
Glamorous Hors d'Oeuvres	Appetizer	Brunch offerings	67
Turkey Agrodolce with a Curry Splash	Poultry	Main course	67
Country Captain Chicken	Poultry	Main course	68
Savory Steak	Steak	Meat, main course	68

ZANY JELLIES, PICKLES and THEN SOME	Category	Use(s)	Page No.
Beth's Farm Kitchen Mighty Hot Pepper Jelly	Jelly		70
A Bagel Treat: Sunday Morning Special	Breakfast		70
Beth's Farm Kitchen Habanero Jelly	Jelly		71
Beth's Farm Kitchen Garlic Jelly	Jelly		72
Garlic Bruschetta	Appetizer		72
Salad Dressing	Dressing	Marinade	73
Beth's Farm Kitchen Garlic-Rosemary Jelly	Jelly		73
Garlic Gingery Pear Chicken	Main dish	Chicken	74
Veggie Kabobs	Vegetables	Vegetarian, vegan	74
Garlic-Rosemary BBQ Spare Ribs	Meat	Appetizer, spare ribs	75
Beth's Farm Kitchen Spicy Corn Relish	Relish		76
Spicy, Cheesy Corn Bread	Bread	Side dish	77
Beth's Farm Kitchen Bread & Butter Pickles	Pickles		78
Cuban Sandwich	Main dish	Brunch, lunch	79
Beth's Farm Kitchen Adapt-a-Recipe for Dilly Beans, Dilly Carrots and Veggies	Pickled vegetables	Vegetarian, vegan	80
The Perfect Sushi Pretender	Appetizer	Vegetarian, vegan, picnic food	81
Beth's Farm Kitchen Red Tomato Jam	Jam		82
Romeo's Curried Chicken	Main dish	Chicken	82

Jam Notes

Questions? Contact bfk@bethsfarmkitchen.com

Questions? Contact bfk@bethsfarmkitchen.com